EMPIRE AND SUPEREMPIRE

EMPIRE AND SUPEREMPIRE

BRITAIN, AMERICA AND THE WORLD

BERNARD PORTER

YALE UNIVERSITY PRESS
NEW HAVEN AND LONDON

For information about this and other Yale University Press publications, please contact:
U.S. Office: sales.press@yale.edu   yalebooks.com
Europe Office: sales@yaleup.co.uk   www.yaleup.co.uk

Set in Minion by J&L Composition, Filey, North Yorkshire
Printed in Great Britain by St Edmundsbury Press Ltd, Bury St Edmunds

Library of Congress Cataloging-in-Publication Data

Porter, Bernard.
Empire and superempire: Britain, America, and the world/Bernard Porter.
   p.cm.
   Includes bibliographical references and index.
   ISBN 0–300–11010–3 (cl.: alk. paper)
1. United States–Foreign relations–2001-2. Great Britain–Foreign relations–1997-3. United States–Foreign relations. 4. Great Britain–Foreign relations. 5. United States–Colonial question. 6. Great Britain–Colonies–History. 7. Imperialism–History. I. Title.
E895.P67 2006
   325'.320973090511–dc22

2005034780

A catalogue record for this book is available from the British Library.

10 9 8 7 6 5 4 3 2 1

Contents

Acknowledgements

I have a few debts to acknowledge. The main libraries I have used in my reading for this book are Kungliga Biblioteket in Stockholm – amazingly well stocked with British and American books, and a delightful place to work; the University Library in Cambridge; and the British Library at St Pancras. Living in exile as I do, away from British bookshops, Amazon.co.uk, AbeBooks.co.uk and Google.com have also helped. It was Heather McCallum at Yale University Press who suggested I write this book; I am grateful to her for that, for her bold and wise advice throughout the preliminary stages of setting it up, and for her support all the way through. Philip Harling, one of her 'readers', also contributed critically and very helpfully. (It goes without saying that these advisors are in no way responsible for what is written here, especially those bits I've left in against their advice.) My current Swedish surroundings have given me a new perspective on Anglo-American history (the Swedes haven't been imperialists, at least in any obvious way, for ages), and Kajsa has been a wonderful critical sounding-board. My thanks to them all.

All essential citations appear in a 'Sources and references' section at the end.

Bernard Porter
Enskede/Svartsö
September 2005

Introduction

Denial

Most modern Americans are insistent that they 'don't do empire', as Donald Rumsfeld put it once. This is while they are doing all kinds of things that to other people look uncommonly like empire, such as invading countries, changing their governments and dominating them in various ways. What Rumsfeld and Co. mean, of course, is that they have no hankering after *formal empire*: don't particularly want to conquer or annex territories, or to rule their peoples directly. Some Americans would claim that what they are doing is the very opposite of imperialism: liberating people, usually from tyrannies; and making the world safer by neutralising those tyrannies' capacities to imperialise others. It is this, they say, that marks America off from all previous empires. One of the empires it is supposed to mark them off from is the British; which they know all about, of course, from historical experience. The United States, after all, owes its origin to a rebellion against this tyrannical empire. This is one of the reasons why it is unlikely to resort to an imperialism of its own today.

Personally, I'm not one of those who would automatically dismiss Rumsfeld's and other Americans' rejection of the 'imperial' tag for themselves on these grounds. The modern American empire *is* different from all others in history, including the British, and, in its rhetoric at any rate, can claim to be more benevolent than most. (That is not to say that it is necessarily more bene*ficent*: we'll be coming to this difference later on.) It may even be wrong to call it an empire, though that is more a matter of semantics than anything else. 'Empire' and 'imperialism' are contentious terms, as every student of history and politics knows. Their meanings have shifted over time. 'Empire' used to be defined in terms of clear and overt rule by one nation over others; in late nineteenth-century British terms, for instance, exemplified in the parts that were coloured red on those famous world maps. Later this came to seem an inadequate way of characterising 'imperialism', as it left out all kinds of control across national boundaries that were every bit as confining as this 'formal' kind of empire, even though they were only indirect. Rumsfeld and Co. don't seem to have reached this stage of thinking yet. But there are genuine problems with it. Once you leave the clearly fenced-off field of 'formal rule' to go into the more open and disputed territory of 'informal empire', *judgements* come into play. The word empire, from its etymology, must surely imply 'power' by one people over another; but the amount and kind of power in any of these situations can be controversial. This has led to an enormous proliferation of the ways the term is taken in recent years, some of which are – at the very least – less than useful. It is fairly common today, for example, to talk of American cultural influence (McDonald's, jeans, Hollywood movies) as 'imperialism'. Unless all these things have been forced on people, that seems to me to be ridiculous. But that is only my view. 'Imperialism' is only a word. You can use it any way you like (so long as you make that usage clear). Personally, I prefer a definition that goes beyond Rumsfeld's implied one; but his is as valid as any. It has the advantage for him, of course, of automatically letting America off the 'imperialist' hook for most of her history. I don't object to that; so long as he (if he ever reads this, which of course is unlikely) will do the same for some of the characteristics of British imperialism, which were similar to what he denies is 'imperialism' in the modern American case.

This is what has impressed me, and many of my fellow British imperial historians, about recent events in Afghanistan, Iraq and elsewhere. The parallels with certain aspects of British imperial history are just too glaring to ignore. Afghanistan and Iraq, of course, were both famous sites of British imperialism: the first as one of the main arenas of the nineteenth-century 'Great Game' between Britain and Russia over the control of central and south Asia; the second as a territory that was 'mandated' to Britain – virtually a colony – after the First World War. You can probably still see British soldiers' boot prints there if you look carefully. That is certainly true metaphorically in the case of Iraq. (Britain created the country.) There are other parallels. 'Gladstone in Egypt' (1882) is one that occurred to several of us, as a precedent for 'Bush in Iraq' (2003). It's nearly all there: a great power marching in to rescue a people from tyranny and mismanagement; the commitment to leave as soon as the job is done; suspected economic motives; an assertive Islam; Christian religiosity on the Western side; international difficulties (especially with France); and a national uprising that eventually keeps Britain bogged down in Egypt, against her original intention. Be warned, George W.! Of course these similarities *are* only superficial. Other parallels, however, are closer. One has to do with the rhetoric used in both cases. America claims she isn't acting imperially; that she intervenes only reluctantly, and under pressure of necessity; and that her motives are of the best: the spread of 'freedom' (the word repeated thirty-seven times in Bush's 2005 Inaugural Address) in the world. It may surprise some people to learn that Britain regarded her foreign policy during most of the nineteenth century in almost exactly the same way. It is easily possible to imagine Gladstone saying 'we don't do empire', even while he was in the process of invading Egypt, if he had had Rumsfeld's talent for the short, direct phrase. If it is fair to describe America as an 'empire', then she isn't the first one in history to be in denial.

The 'denial' thing does not apply to all Americans. Radicals among them, for example, have regarded their country as 'imperialist' for years. This usually refers to her commercial and financial presence in the world, some of which would certainly qualify as 'imperialism' in my book (if an element of coercion could be shown), but which Rumsfeld presumably genuinely could not see as such. (This is another thing he had in common with nineteenth-century Britons.) This, of course, is using the 'i'-word disparagingly, which is the usual way these days. It is a popular way of looking at American foreign policy by its critics in Europe, also.

Recently, however, another kind of American has appeared, or rather reappeared (we shall come across some earlier examples later), who has also grasped the nettle, but rather likes the feel of it. This is the school of political ideologues known as 'neoconservatives', who see the twenty-first century as essentially 'America's', when her power and ideals will dominate in the world, much as they see British power and ideals having domi nated in the nineteenth century. They do not always call it by the 'i'-word, presumably for fear of alienating their compatriots. The squeamish, wrote the columnist Mark Steyn, could 'give it some wussified Clinto-Blairite name like "global community outreach"' if they liked; but it was still imperialism, he claimed, and all the better for it. Some, however, are bolder. 'People are now coming out of the closet on the word "empire",' noticed right-wing commentator Charles Krauthammer early in 2002. Sure enough: 'I prefer the more forthright if also more controversial term American Empire', said former Bush speechwriter David Frum a little later, ' – sort of like the way some gays embrace the "queer" label.' Accepting the word 'imperial' enables them to consider positively other imperial precedents. The two most common ones are the Roman, and the British. (Very few take up the Spanish example, or the 'evil' Soviet one, though there are points of resemblance here too.) The British Empire seems particularly attractive. What 'Afghanistan and other troubled lands today cry out for', wrote the columnist Max Boot in 2001, was 'the sort of enlightened foreign administration once provided by self-confident Englishmen in jodhpurs and pith helmets'. Broadly speaking, that is also the Harvard historian Niall Ferguson's line, in his fine *Colossus: The Rise and Fall of the American Empire* (2004), which urges America to follow Britain's example more closely and committedly. (I disagree with this, but mainly because my emphasis is different: less on power and economics than on the human, social and cultural sides of empire.) Incidentally, most of these commentators were not American-born, which may say something about the continued taboo status of the word in the broader culture of America. Interestingly, this is yet another thing that modern American imperialism shares with its British forerunner.

The old British Empire, therefore, has already been used to point useful 'lessons' for present-day America, either as a cautionary warning, or as an example to imitate. This book, generally, will not seek to do that. Like most academic historians – it is what makes us so use*less* – I am reluctant to draw direct lessons from history in this kind of way. Events are always the products of their own times and the conditions surrounding them. Superficial parallels can be misleading, even dangerously so, if they are leant on too much. An example is the use that is still often made of spurious Second World War precedents to justify actions (especially wars), which in the case of the Iraq War may actually have led to loss of life. How many American soldiers, for example – and more Iraqi civilians – died because Rumsfeld believed they would be greeted in the streets of Baghdad by cheering girls waving flowers, just as the GIs had been in Paris in 1944? Egypt (1882) might have been a better precedent to look to in that situation. Obviously the Americans were reluctant to pick that, because it was a colonial one. Even if they had, however, there is no guarantee that it could have helped them much more. History never repeats itself precisely. The best lesson that can be drawn from it is not to try to draw lessons from it like this.

Themes

It is in this spirit that this book has been written. It originally arose out of my irritation at the way the history of the British Empire has been 'used' on both sides of the debate over modern American (and British) foreign policy, without very much understanding, it seems to me, of what it really was. This lack of understanding is clear in nearly every book that has been written recently about American 'imperialism' which mentions the British precedent, whether in order to distance the former from it, or to use it as a model. (It is interesting, incidentally, how many 'big books' have come out of America recently on this kind of theme, many with broad sweeps, grand theories and 'colossal' titles – *The End of History*; *The Clash of Civilizations*; *The Dynamics of Global Dominance*; and so on; another echo of Britain's imperial age. This may be a side-effect of great empires – to produce empire-sized explanations for things.) With regard to the British precedent, there are some exceptions. Ferguson's book is a notable one. (He had prepared for it by writing another one *on* the British Empire.) Clyde Prestowitz, in his much more critical *Rogue Nation* (2003), though he doesn't make much of the comparison, usually gets it right when he does. Others, however, don't. One common error is to conflate the British with other contemporary and even non-contemporary imperialisms, in a general, all-purpose, generally caricatured stereotype. It is this that blinds many commentators to the parallels that might be drawn between America's and Britain's imperialisms *in particular*, as well as to some of the real and vital differences. It also leads them to draw some of those false 'lessons' for today; which concern me, both as a citizen (and of the nation most closely allied to US 'imperialism'), and as a historian who hates to see people distorting the past, and especially 'my' past – the area I have been researching and writing about for years, that is – in this way. (I admit to this personal interest.) This book will aim to correct some of those distortions; and then to discuss the implications of a more accurate – or at least, a more complex and sophisticated – view of British imperialism for the comparison with present-day America. If there are lessons to be drawn from historical comparisons, we ought at least to try to get the latter right.

In fact they are uncannily close in this case. In the first place, America was at least *as* imperialist as Britain throughout her history as a nation – from the very time, that is, when they split apart – despite her obstinate insistence for much of that period that she was not imperialist at all, by *contrast* with Britain. This is not a new argument. Niall Ferguson makes it, for one, forcefully and effectively. So do many of America's present-day critics. I imagine that most American academic historians these days accept – they must do – that America has been at least a little bit imperialist for much of the past 200 years. My case, however, goes beyond this. As well as being *as* imperialist as Britain, America was also imperialist in most of the same ways. This may surprise those who hold that American imperialism, if it is to be called that, was (and is) nonetheless qualitatively different from and (by implication) better than all other imperialisms, including the hated British; that it was, to use the word most commonly applied to this kind of thinking on the part of Americans, 'exceptional'. On the contrary, it was until recently very ordinary; close to the imperialisms of all other contemporary powers, but especially close to nineteenth-century Britain's.

In a way, that latter imperialism could be regarded as a *dry run* for the modern American variety; which is one reason why Americans, and all of us, should perhaps pay more attention to it. In order to see this, however, we need to have a clearer idea about what British imperialism really was, as against the popular images of it (on both sides of the Atlantic), which engender so many of those misleading comparisons and contrasts. One thing we will find is that it was in some ways *less* 'imperialistic' than those images; which may make the comparison easier for some Americans to swallow. In other words, American imperialism is closer than we think to the British kind because the British kind was closer than we think to the American. (Incidentally: this should not be taken as intending to *excuse* the British Empire in any way. This book will not be an apologia for it; or, for that matter, the opposite. I feel I need to make this clear at the start, as it is my experience that anti-imperialists often jump to this conclusion about any new 'revisions' of imperial history that come along.) This forms the main theme of Chapter 1.

Chapter 2 then places the template of the first two centuries of American 'imperialism' over this, in order to see how it fits. This is probably the least original section of the book, as I've indicated already; but it does make one or two new points, which turn out to be significant later on. These are mainly to do with those places where the template *doesn't* quite fit; where American imperialism, or, more often, the broader American society, exhibits slight peculiarities, which then become magnified. The full magnification comes in very modern times; which is what Chapter 3 is about. All the ingredients of post-9/11 American imperialism can be traced back to earlier times; but after that date they were suddenly pushed to the forefront. It was then that American imperialism for the first time *transcended* its British predecessor; became something far greater – if it works, that is; if not, then far more hubristic. I call this 'superempire'. Again, this needs to be spelled out, because it may not be as widely appreciated as it should be. Just as Americans tend to think they are more different from Europeans than they really are ('exceptional'), so many Europeans, especially Britons, assume they are more similar. America sprang from our loins, after all; was largely peopled by Britons; and speaks our language (roughly). It is natural to think of her as an extension of 'British' or 'European' or 'Western' civilisation basically. But that hides some crucial differences, as many of us, I think, came to realise after the 2000 and 2004 Presidential elections (the results of which seemed literally inexplicable to most typical secular, liberal, rationalist Europeans); some of which have affected the recent course of America's empire profoundly. American imperialism today *is* different from the old British kind; not in the ways Americans themselves tend to believe (more reluctant, more benevolent – *less* imperialistic, perhaps), but in other and much more crucial respects. We shall come on to these. Here the *contrasts* between the two imperialisms may be as suggestive as the parallels I shall also be drawing.

Much of this 'new' imperialism, of course, was implemented in close harness with one of the 'old' imperial powers (or rather, with its leader); which raises some interesting questions of its own. Did British imperialism really die when it is supposed to have done? Is there a concrete link between the two forms of imperialism? Or a common – 'Anglo-Saxon', say – set of characteristics? As well as this, however, the link also illustrates some of the differences between the American and British approaches that will have emerged in the first three chapters; for, as I shall be showing, Bush and Blair were not in fact the complete soulmates they often portrayed themselves as (in the interests of unity) during their common endeavours in Afghanistan and Iraq. Chapter 4 is devoted to this. After that comes a final chapter pulling all this together, or trying to, and reaching some general conclusions.

Among those conclusions there will not be many practical 'lessons', as I've indicated already; and no firm predictions at all. (Just one tentative one.) As a historian, I don't consider myself to be in that business. I don't claim that the outcome in modern Iraq can be foretold from the Egyptian precedent, for example; or want to advise the American government to start buying in supplies of jodhpurs and pith helmets to help it run the place. (Actually the British did not wear jodhpurs when they were *ruling*.) Nonetheless, I do believe a comparison between these two empires may be enlightening in many ways. It should dispel some myths and misunderstandings which are sometimes used today to bolster political attitudes and decisions, on both sides of the Atlantic, for one. By bringing British and American history closer together, it may help counter the rather worrying – I think – modern American myth of 'exceptionalism' generally: that America is somehow different from and better than anywhere else. She *is* different, but no more than any nation is different from others; and mainly in her *belief* in her exceptionalism, not the reality of it, certainly in this field. It may be helpful for Americans to know that other countries – in this case Britain – have trodden this 'imperial' path before them: that in other words, they are just like any nation in this regard. It may also, without giving clear answers to any of the questions and diffi- culties that are bound to arise in their quest for a new world order, suggest a range of alternatives which won't occur to someone who believes that he or she is alone and first. As well as this, it must be instructive to know which features of modern American 'imperialism' *are* distinctive, and puzzle and perhaps shock other peoples; that is, the characteristics of it that really do mark the American empire off from others, rather than those that are merely supposed to. For analysts, it clearly raises inter- esting questions: if two historical phenomena, however far apart, appear so similar, might there not be some common factors behind them both? In the case of British and American imperialism in the nineteenth century the broad imperatives behind them both become clearer if we bracket them together, I think, than if we treat each event as *sui generis*.

Lastly, there is a further intriguing possibility. As well as similarities, there are clear *connections* between the old British Empire and the new American one. One runs in to the other. In many ways the Americans, after the Second World War, took up where the British left off. Were these the same phenomenon, essentially? An 'Anglo-Saxon-Celtic' empire, perhaps, dominating the whole period from the nineteenth century to the twenty-first, albeit in different garbs? (I include the Celts here because, although it suits the Irish and Scots now to present themselves as victims of British imperialism, they were in fact as much complicit in it as the English.) There is a superficial allure to this. There is even a 'conspiracy theory' to explain it: it involves a secret society of British imperialists that managed to infiltrate the American political establishment throughout the twentieth century. (Look out for 'Rhodes Scholars'.) I should warn aficionados of this kind of explanation that I shan't be giving much quarter to this idea in this book, or to the 'racial' – Anglo-Saxon-Celtic – one; but the broader question, of the actual *links* between the two empires, does deserve some attention. That will be discussed here too.

Problems

I wrote this book as a contribution to a current political debate, though I hope its value may outlast the events that inspired it. It is, therefore, the first of my books that has a frankly polemical agenda, albeit – as I have just tried to indicate – a mainly negative one. That is, it seeks to undermine *other* polemics by showing how wrong or simplistic the historical assumptions behind many of them are. But I do have more positive views on these matters, which I have not sought to repress (or hide) as much as in my other writings. They should be quite apparent therefore in the following pages; apart from one, which has a general import, and so may be worth singling out for mention.

This is the strong personal aversion I have to the idea and sentiment of 'patriotism' – which is not to say that I cannot understand it (I think). I believe that pride in one's country is irrational, and pride in its *history* even more so; simply because one's nationality is usually a matter of luck (except for immigrants), and no one living today can be credited with – or, it follows from this, held to blame for – anything that happened in his or her country's more distant past. I also think that patriotism, or nationalism – it is sometimes difficult to separate them – is more often dangerous than not. That obviously prejudices me against present-day displays of American patriotism; the other side of the coin, however, is that I am not likely to favour Britain, my own country, in the comparisons I shall be making between the two nations' 'imperialisms', on these grounds. In fact I feel no pride whatsoever in being British (as opposed to *grateful* – which is something entirely different – for having been raised in a land that has cricket, medieval village churches, and steak and kidney puddings). Nor do I believe that I am generally anti-American. My attitude towards the United States, which I know well, is in fact similar to my view of most other countries in the world (including the 'model' social democracy I currently live in): ambivalent, deeply admiring of many aspects, but critical of others. That may not be good enough for the most patriotic Americans, but it is reasonable, I think, and as much as one should expect from a sceptical academic. If there are mistakes in the American sections of this book, therefore, they will not have arisen from any kind of all-purpose anti-Americanism on my part.

So far as the British side is concerned, it is less likely that I have made mistakes, because that is where my main expertise lies; but there will certainly be some, for which I apologise in advance;

and it is only fair to point out that some of my *judgements* are controversial. This is particularly so in relation to the domestic impact and importance of British imperialism, which are germane to my general argument; where I shall be stating conclusions that I have aired before, but only recently, in my last book before this one, which means that they haven't yet had time to be properly tested. Most of my other ideas on the British side of the picture have seen the light of day previously in other books and articles of mine, in particular *The Lion's Share: A Short History of British Imperialism 1850–2004* (4th edn, 2004); indeed, I may even have unwittingly repeated some phrases from there. On the other hand, the American comparison which is the main theme of the present book puts a different slant on the picture all through. It has also, incidentally, changed my own views in certain ways, as 'comparative' studies are almost bound to do. 'What should they know of England, who only England know,' wrote Rudyard Kipling once. He meant something entirely different (it was an injunction to get out there and learn about the *Empire*); but I have always thought it would make a good motto for those who, like myself, believe you can never properly know your own country's history in isolation. That is a good argument for this book, whoever is the reader. If she is a Briton wanting to understand Britain's imperial history, the American context will aid her; if he is an American eager to get to the bottom of the invasion of Iraq in 2003, the British perspective should help him, too.

Lastly, and trivially, a couple of points about language. The first is that I use the word 'America' throughout this book to refer to the United States alone. This of course is strictly wrong, but it is common practice, and makes things easier in many situations: for example, when talking about 'Americ*ans*'. The second is that I use the feminine pronoun ('she', 'her', 'hers') to refer not only to America, but also to all other nations; which I understand is falling out of fashion now, and is disapproved of in some quarters. I can see no objection to it; more to the point, most feminists I have talked to about this cannot either. (Perhaps it's the masculinists who object?) I think it sounds better, and in some contexts makes things clearer: when, for example, 'it' might refer back to a number of other subjects. There are a couple of places in the book where 'she' is inappropriate: where I describe a country metaphorically as doing something (usually nasty) that only a man can do. I've noted this, where it comes up.

Finally, it occurred to me as I was checking this book for the printers that one passage in it might be thought to fall foul of legislation being mooted in Britain at the time to outlaw the defence or 'glorifying' of 'terrorism'. That's where I present terrorism as a rational choice in some circumstances: where, for example, an enemy has an overwhelming conventional military advantage. I hope that doesn't sound too exculpatory. 'Rational' is not always good. For the record, I regard 'terrorism', whatever its provenance – and that includes state terrorism, of course – as always evil. There: that should cover me. (Though I'm not sure I know what 'evil' means.)

This book isn't mainly about terrorism, however. It's about 'imperialism'. Its main aim is to *problemetize* that concept, applied especially to American foreign policy – to inform and, hopefully, sophisticate the debate. If readers come out of it feeling much less *certain* than they did about both American and British imperialisms – less willing to apply easy judgements, one way or the other – then it will have done its job.

1

'Like a house of cards'
The British Empire, myth and reality

Appearances

Most people have got the wrong idea about the British Empire. It is usually seen as a vast system of control in the world, immensely powerful, founded on British strength, fuelled by acquisitiveness, both for commercial profits and for territory, riding roughshod over foreign societies and cultures, a matter of great pride for the British people, and deeply racist. Either that, or it was a means of spreading modernity and civilisation into the dark places of the earth. This is a less common view today – it used to be more so, of course, at the Empire's height – but it has shown signs of reviving recently, for example with Niall Ferguson's *Empire: How Britain Made the Modern World* (2002). The former view is far more widespread, especially abroad. There are elements of truth in both these pictures. The British Empire was powerful, racist, proselytising, popular and all the rest to some degree, and at various times. But none of these characterisations, or even a combination of them, describes the essence of it. To see the British Empire in these simplistic terms is to misunderstand it utterly.

It is easy to see how it has come to appear like this. For a start, the very word 'empire' implies dominion over others – comes from a Latin root, indeed, which means just that. Secondly, look at all those maps of the British Empire that are so familiar to us from the later nineteenth century: vast swathes of bright red scattered over every portion of the globe, exaggerating the extent of the empire to a degree, perhaps, in Mercator's projection, which stretches the icy wastes of northern Canada out on the top left rather, but still pretty impressive. Red is a deeply dominating colour. Thirdly, at that time – the late nineteenth century – the British Empire did, briefly, take on some of these characteristics that are usually associated with it today: purposely land-grabbing, backed by a degree of national pride ('jingoism'), professing a 'civilising mission', and so on. Most of our images of the Empire come from this period. They are more accurate for that time than for any other. Fourthly, it was in the interests of British imperialists, who always of course existed, to project the Empire in this powerful way. For a start, it helped them to hold on to it. It deterred their colonial subjects from rebelling against it (though not always). It also puffed themselves up. Strutting around their governors' mansions in gold-laced uniforms and plumed hats, or lording it over the 'natives' in their pith helmets and khaki shorts, made them feel part of something important. (They soon came down to earth when they returned to Britain, where they were generally disregarded.) So this was the image they gave out. Fifthly, it was *as* an empire that Britain mainly impinged on the rest of the world. Most foreigners in the nineteenth century were aware of Britain either as their colonial master, or as an imperial rival. To Americans at different times she was both. In the latter case their perception of British impe-rialism is also distorted by its place in their national myth (the War of Independence), which has stuck it in a kind of time warp. Popular Hollywood films like *The Patriot* (2000), with Mel Gibson bravely pitted against King George's proto-Nazis, buttress this. Sixthly, this is of course what many British and Americans – and not only critics – want to believe. The British Empire *needs* to have been powerful in order to have delivered the benefits that have been credited to it by some, or, alternatively, to be responsible for the damage it is supposed to have done. Lastly, there was India. That *was* real. It is scarcely surprising, then, that so many people, especially foreigners, should have this 'big' idea of the British Empire. One should not expect anything else.

The real picture, however, is subtly different. Appearances were deceptive. The motives behind British imperialism were more mixed, its spirit more ambivalent, and its impact more uneven than any of the popular versions of it – both pro and anti – would suggest. This doesn't of course mean that it was either 'better' or 'worse' than those versions have it; only, perhaps, that it may have been 'good' or 'bad' – beneficent or maleficent in its effects – for different reasons. This obviously has a relevance for any parallels or lessons we wish to draw from it for the present day. Some will be less close or apposite than is often assumed. Others may turn out to be more so.

Varieties of empire

It was only towards the end of the nineteenth century that the idea began to be widely propagated that the Victorian Empire was something remarkable or 'great'. That's when those red-bespattered world maps first came on to the scene. Before then, few people had ever thought of colour-coding the Empire in this way. In fact, a majority of Britons probably hardly noticed it. This is not a fashionable view today, especially among a certain kind of scholar that over the past few years has tried to show that Britain was thoroughly soaked in 'imperialism' throughout the nineteenth century; but that is not so. (We shall return to this.) It may also seem counter-intuitive. How could such a huge enterprise as the British Empire – as revealed by those later maps – *not* have been obvious to all Britons, and indeed supported by them? The answer is simple. It did not need to impact on them, at least in any direct and straightforward way. This was because of how it was won, and the way it was ruled.

The nineteenth-century Empire was made up of four broad kinds of colonies. (Later, after the First World War, another one – 'mandates' – was added to these.) The first was India. This had been acquired gradually in the seventeenth and eighteenth centuries, as a result of British trade in the East. Its origin was the famous British East India Company of 1600, a private enterprise but with a Crown monopoly, which began encroaching politically thereafter, mainly to safeguard its trade against both locals and other European (especially French) rivals. To this end it organised its own army, entirely separate from the British – even their personnel was not interchangeable – composed very largely of Indian native lower ranks, or 'sepoys'. The greatest triumph of that army came in 1757, when it defeated an Indian force at Plassey in Bengal fairly easily. Obviously this situation – a commercial company running more and more of a *country* – was liable to abuse, and so the British government took increasing control of its political functions from 1773 on. In 1858, after the rebellion which was the first of the two major challenges to British imperial control in this period, the Company was abolished entirely. Strictly speaking, India only became a British colony then, though it would be pedantic to insist on this. It also came to impinge on British public consciousness, to a limited extent, almost for the first time. It is interesting, however, that the new British *raj* never called itself a 'colony', but always insisted it was an 'empire' in its own right (an Anglo-Indian one), which is why it had a separate Office in London running it; that the separation of the Indian Army from the British Army continued even after 1858; and that many Britons considered Britain's autocratic rule there to be somehow anomalous, out of (national) character. A common way of looking at India in this period was as the unfortunate issue of a liaison entered into in less enlightened or moral times, which Britain would certainly not have mothered if she had been in the same situation today. Again, we should not make too much of this. Britain ruled India – no doubt about it. But it was not a straightforward kind of rule. Nor was it one that impacted on stay-at-home Britons very greatly. Even at the end of the nineteenth century, for example, only about 2,000 men (always men, of course) were required to administer it. They generally formed a caste of their own, who kept apart from other Britons even when they returned 'home'. (Many, in fact, never returned to Britain, regarding their real 'home' as Anglo-India.) Nor did India *cost* the British people. One strict rule for all of the British colonies – not just India – was that they had to support themselves. (That included the cost of the Indian Army.) So the British did not *need* to be aware of it.

The second kind of British colony was also a legacy from less enlightened times. This was the plantation colonies of the Caribbean, acquired (again) from the seventeenth century onwards, or else as booty from the recent French wars. The Southern States of America had once come into this category too; but now, of course, they were 'free'. A characteristic of both (and of one or two other colonies) was that they used slave labour from Africa; which was another reason why the more enlightened nineteenth-century Britons generally disapproved of them too. In 1833 enlightenment prevailed, in Britain if not in 'free' America, when slavery was abolished Empire-wide. (It is a curious irony, which contemporaries were fond of pointing out, that if America had not split from the British Empire in 1783 slavery might have been abolished there too thirty years before Lincoln's final Emancipation Proclamation of 1863.) Thereafter there was no real rationale for Britain to keep the West Indies; but keep them she felt she had to. Again, the 'mother' analogy fits well here: Britain could not just abandon her unfortunate progeny while they still needed her care and protection. 'They' meant both the blacks and the whites there, who were felt to be in danger from one another. The fear of 'race war' was a prime one at the time, and with reason – there *were* racial conflicts, not only in the British West Indies, but also in neighbouring countries (like Haiti). This, however, made their possession of these old plantation colonies a burdensome responsibility in the eyes of most Britons, rather than a matter of pride. It was also a responsibility that was addressed minimally, as in India, with a tiny number of administrators. If anything the West Indies impinged even less on metropolitan Britain than did India. (Of course both countries impinged materially: with sugar and tea, for example; but most people probably didn't realise this.) As well as this – and this is important for British people's *perceptions* of themselves as an imperial nation – neither represented the 'imperialism' of the present (nineteenth-century) day.

That was represented by two other kinds of empire. The first was empire by 'settlement'. That was the sort of empire that had produced the northernmost of the British American colonies in the seventeenth and eighteenth centuries, of course, as well as parts of the South; and which in the nineteenth century gave rise to British Australia, New Zealand, the Cape in South Africa, and the further expansion of those North American colonies that remained loyal to Britain (today's Canada). Most of this settlement, too, was what today we would call 'private enterprise'; very little of it involved any kind of initiative or plan hatched by the British state. Indeed, hardly *any* Colonial Office staff were employed here. When the Colonial Office was brought in it was usually to defend its nationals if they got into trouble, either by force or by diplomacy; or, occasionally, to rein them back. This was supposed to make a difference at the time. Settlement was not regarded as the same as 'imperialism'; rather, it was natural, the spread of enterprising individuals into the 'waste places' of the earth (we shall come on to the problematic aspects of this later), and of the principles of British 'freedom' – because the Britons who settled in Australia and elsewhere effectively governed themselves. (Convicts were an obvious exception, at least until the expiry of their terms. Transportation was stopped in 1869.) In a way, settlement, or 'colonisation', seemed the opposite of 'empire'; certainly if you regarded the latter word as implying some kind of dominance. Many Victorians were aware of *that* – emigration was constantly being urged on the working classes, for example, to solve social problems at home; and might even be proud of it, if they didn't resent being forced to emigrate there just to stay alive. Those that were, were usually just as proud of the United States as of the colonies as extensions of this kind of British freedom and enterprise in the world. They also accepted that Australia and the rest would probably go America's way ultimately. In other words, they did not feel they still had to own it in order to take pride in it.

The last characteristic sort of British colony before the later nineteenth century was the trading posts and naval stations that were found scattered nearly all over the world then – almost as numerous as US air force bases today. These too were not thought to represent 'imperialism' *really*. They were the outcome of Britain's expanding commerce in the eighteenth and nineteenth centuries; a process which was – rather like 'settlement' – not considered to be 'imperialistic' at all. This was especially so after her enactment of 'free trade' in the second quarter of the nineteenth century, which was supposed to remove any 'imperialist' stigma from her commerce entirely. The reason for that was that in the past colonialism had been intimately associated with 'mercantilism', also often called the 'colonial system', which was the opposite of this; from which it followed that if that aspect of trade were taken away, the 'colonialism' must disappear too. Colonialism meant coercion. 'Free trade' was – what its name said – 'free'. I sell; you buy – openly and willingly. Where could be the 'imperialism' in that? Of course, you couldn't have free trade – or trade of any sort – without certain basic political and economic conditions being met. Your traders needed security, for example, both bodily and financial (they shouldn't have to run the risks of being killed or not paid); and also safe harbours, entrepôts and coaling stations for their vessels. This was the origin of most of this fourth kind of 'colony' in the nineteenth century. Most of them started off simply *as* coastal bases, leased perhaps (but not always) from local rulers. Whether these should strictly be called colonies (any more than American airstrips should) is problematical. Sometimes, however, they could grow more colony-like. They could find themselves 'forced' to expand a little way inland, for instance, in order to secure themselves against attack from neighbours. The unsettling impact in their hinterlands of traders and missionaries sometimes compounded this. Later, as we shall see, foreign (European) rivalry induced further expansion. This was how most of them grew into more genuine 'colonies'. On the whole, however, these colonies were marginal *qua* colonies before the 1880s. Most of them are represented on our earlier 'Empire' maps as little red dots; which is all they were. It is easy to understand why people may not have noticed them.

Imperial virginity

There are two points to be made from this. Both run counter to modern popular views of the British Empire in the nineteenth century. They also have an important bearing on any comparison we may wish to make with modern American 'imperialism'. The first point is that however imperial *we* may feel the early and mid Victorians were, many of them will not have agreed. They were deluded, of course, but the delusion is a significant one. Secondly, the British Empire – even if we accept its existence then, as we must – was in many ways a much lesser affair than it is sometimes taken to have been. It took less trouble both to acquire and to rule, for example. This is one of the reasons why contemporaries didn't feel particularly imperialist. But it also had a much more important rider. It meant, as we shall see shortly, that it was always fundamentally weak.

This belief in their national virginity *vis-à-vis* empire is one of the surprising things about the early and mid Victorians; especially in view of all the signs of inchastity that lay around them – not only old India and the British West Indies, but also the new young colonies she spawned in every decade of this period. It is why, of course, many modern scholars simply don't believe it. One reason for it was semantic; another was ideological. The *word* imperialism was usually applied to something entirely different at this time: the pretensions of the tyrant Bonaparte, and then, later, of his much despised nephew Napoleon III, who both *called* themselves 'Emperors'. That association made it a taboo word in Britain for most of the century, much as its association with Britain and, even more, the 'evil' empire of the Soviets makes it a taboo word in the USA today. The other main reason was ideological. In broad terms, Britain thought of herself as a 'free' country (again like modern America), and empire was the opposite of 'freedom'. As we have just seen, it was the opposite of free *trade* in particular. This went back to Adam Smith, who was the one who had first developed the theory that free trade was the best means to *The Wealth of Nations* (the title of his great book), and so seemed to undermine completely the economic rationale, at any rate, for empire. By happy coincidence *The Wealth of Nations* was published in the very year the American colonists gave formal notice of their intention to quit the British Empire (1776). By even happier coincidence, one effect of that was that Britain's trade with her American ex-colonies substantially increased thereafter, which seemed to prove Smith's point.

The free market capitalist objection to imperialism, however, went much deeper than this. Imperialism was a form of government; and all government – according to the high priests of the faith – was at best a regrettable necessity, and generally a Bad

Thing. It could only stifle enterprise. (The purists had no idea that it might stimulate it, too.) It diverted bright young men into unprofitable pursuits: activities, that is, that were not increasing the national (and of course their own) wealth. It cost money, which could only be raised by taxes, which – again – deducted from the capital that could be being invested in industry and trade. The idea of taxing people to help commerce – to stake out its markets for it, for example – was ridiculous; something akin to killing (or at least confining) the goose that was laying the golden eggs. The best kind of economy was a low tax, entrepreneurial one. Empires seemed inconsistent with that. As well as this, according to Richard Cobden, the highest political priest of free trade in the mid-nineteenth century, it was bound to bring imperialism to its knees where it did still exist. Because free trade flourished best in conditions of amity and freedom, its ultimate tendency would be the eradication of 'large and mighty empires' – all of them, not only Britain's – and the liberation and unification of the whole of humanity 'in the bonds of eternal peace', no less. It went without saying that the *process* of this would be peaceful as well; Cobdenites, unlike some later ideological free traders, were not in the business of forcing free markets on people. It would all be done through 'enlightenment'. Others saw trade carrying 'civilisation' into those parts of the world that were not yet 'civilised'. Hence David Livingstone's famous plea to his compatriots to open up Africa to 'Christianity, commerce and civilisation', which is sometimes taken as revealing the truly sordid motives of Britain's 'civilising mission', simply by bracketing the three together; but this does scant justice to contemporaries' genuine belief in trade as a force for moral good. They may have been ideologically gullible, these Victorians, but they were not hypocrites; or at least, do not need to have been.

Present-day enthusiasts for 'globalisation' (which is what Cobden was essentially preaching) could scarcely view it more optimistically. Nowadays of course globalisation is seen as problematical in many quarters, and as an equivalent of imperialism in some. The difficulty arises mainly from the inequalities that exist in the international trading community, making 'weak' economies vulnerable to 'strong' ones, or currently to 'multinational companies'; thus negating what is theoretically supposed to be the main benefit of free trade, which is to enrich everyone. The market can also be 'rigged' to the advantage of its stronger participants. All this creates a situation of domination and exploitation which is similar to the 'imperial' one. We can see that (or the possibility of it) today. In mid nineteenth-century Britain, however, they generally could not. These were the heady early days of free enterprise doctrine, remember, when it was supposed by some to provide the answer to all the world's problems – including inequality, incidentally; there was a strong strain of the theory that held it would eventually narrow down economic and social differences within society – a far cry from today – and was objected to by hardly anyone. This was, to repeat, not 'imperialism', but 'liberation' – the absolute opposite. The Victorians could not have conceived of it in any other way. (They may have been right.) This too chimes in closely with modern American commercial doctrine, of course.

We can see this denial of imperialism in almost every aspect of British domestic culture before around the 1880s, certainly among the middle and working classes (the upper classes were different). Recently a school of thought, usually called 'postcolonial theory', has tried to persuade us otherwise: that the whole of nineteenth-century British society, from beginning to end of the century and from top to bottom, was 'steeped' (or some other such word) in 'imperialism'; but that is simply wrong. (It comes of not reading enough, jumping to conclusions, using words like 'imperialism' loosely, and reading things 'into' texts.) In fact the British Empire was very largely ignored within Britain; rarely seen as a 'whole' – people might have known about Australia, but not connected it with India, for example; and scarcely ever made a matter of pride in the literature of the time at any level. India especially was quite surprisingly neglected, in view of its importance. Imperial matters only impinged when they involved wars (like the Indian 'Mutiny'), and then superficially. Most Britons were far more concerned with other public matters: political reform, emancipation (of Jews, and so on), the domestic impact of capitalism, church questions, crime, education, social status, and simply living. So far as their national self-awareness was concerned, that varied somewhat according to class; but – outside the upper classes – it nearly always featured, at its centre, a pride in British 'liberties'. That, for example, was the main theme of most school history textbooks during the nineteenth century, the ones that established Britain's national mythology among the young: the *progress* of Britain towards domestic 'freedom' from the seventeenth century onwards; which is very similar to the dominant American national myth, except that that is seen as having been grasped (in 1776) all at once. The Empire scarcely appears in this at all; to the irritation, for example, of Sir John Seeley, the great imperial ideologue of the late nineteenth century: to read all these texts, as he wrote in 1883, you would think that the Empire had been acquired 'in a fit of absence of mind'. Of course it hadn't; but this certainly reflects many early and mid Victorians' perception of themselves.

This perception collapsed, of course, towards the end of the nineteenth century. After Britain's imperial shenanigans then – in Egypt, the Sudan, West and East Africa, South Africa, China and a score of other places – no one could doubt any longer the reality of her imperialism. Everyone is aware of the wave of popular enthusiasm for empire that arose then, and peaked around 1898–1900: though its breadth and, especially, its 'depth' are still a matter for debate. (People could just have liked the excitement.) It is worth pointing out, however, that this degree of 'jingoism', as it is called (after a music-hall song of the 1870s), *was* a new phenomenon at this time; and that it fell away sharply during the course of the South African War (1899–1902), which was the occasion for the most extreme manifestations of it – prominent *anti*-war people being set upon by mobs, for example. One of the major repercussions of that war, in fact – we shall return to the war itself shortly – was to provoke an important critical debate over 'imperialism' in the country. J. A. Hobson's *Imperialism: A Study* (1902), the classic anti-imperialist text of the twentieth century – it is usually credited with having invented the 'capitalist theory' of imperialism – was forged in the heat of the war. Anti-imperialism got a great boost. So did 'internationalist' alternatives to imperialism. Many imperialists took fright at this; one in 1909, for example, saw 'Anti-Imperialists of all shades' looming around him, all intent on bringing about 'an appalling catastrophe to the human race – the downfall of the Empire'. He was probably being paranoid; but there can be little doubt that Britain as a whole was not overwhelmingly committed to her empire in the 1900s. The imperialists believed this was a source of weakness. They were right.

Vulnerability

In fact that weakness had always been potentially there. The underlying reason for it was that the Empire was acquired originally relatively easily, and by a predominantly liberal society, which meant that if a time ever came when it needed to be defended more actively and less liberally, Britain would be hard pressed to do it. The settlement colonies, for example, were not always walkovers: there was spirited resistance from native Americans, New Zealand Maoris and several of the southern African peoples (we shall be returning to this); but the inherent technological disparities between these races and the Europeans usually ensured that the latter triumphed in the end. 'Whatever happens we have got /' in the famous (and ironic) words of Hilaire

Belloc, 'The Gatling gun and they have not.' European diseases, to
which these others had no natural immunities, were also a help.
So was the Royal Navy, where it could be used: which usually
meant where it had coasts to bombard. Britain's wars with China
in the 1830s and '50s, which got Hong Kong for her, are the pre-
eminent case of this. They are also, incidentally, the most extreme
nineteenth-century example of 'free trade' metamorphosing into
an obvious imperialism. They were fought because the Chinese
reneged on agreements to allow British imports in. Never mind
that the main import was Indian-grown opium, which the
Chinese government was trying to stop from addling the brains of
its subjects; it was the principle of the thing that mattered. (Many
contemporary Britons condemned the 'Opium Wars' too.) But it
was also comparatively easy. Chinese junks could put up little
resistance against British men o' war. Most of Britain's imperial
conquests were like this.

For those who believe that the extent of British rule in the
world, as illustrated by those world maps, betokened her 'power',
this needs to be borne in mind. In fact the maps are misleading
as a guide to Britain's real strength. They can even be read in a
totally opposite way. Scarcely any of the red patches, note, are in
Europe. This was for a number of reasons, not the least of which
was that Britain did not have any territorial ambitions there.
Even if she had done, however, she would not have been able to
satisfy them. The reason for this was that her military forces
(outside India) were far too weak. Throughout the nineteenth
century, Britain always had a significantly smaller army than
three or four of her European neighbours. This is another reason
why she only once joined in a Continental war between 1815 and
1914, and then (1854–6) with a far stronger military power
(France) at her side. Lord Palmerston's reputation as a 'bully'
derives from the fact that he only sent his gunboats against
smaller powers; everywhere else he relied on diplomacy, multi-
lateralism and the 'balance of power' (among *several* powers), to

uphold Britain's security. The red patches on the map are, in a way, proof of this weakness. They look impressive, but in fact – with a couple of exceptions – they did not take very much effort or strength to control. They were the world's easy pickings at that time. What Britain was practising during most of the nineteenth century was what Emmanuel Todd calls, in relation to modern America, 'micromilitarism': little wars against much weaker enemies. This was not necessarily a sign of power. The bully who picks on the smallest boys in the playground to tyrannise is not displaying his strength thereby, however many bloodied noses he leaves in his wake. It would be different if he squared up to another member of the school football team. But between Napoleon and the Kaiser, Britain never did that. If she was a 'great power', she was a very specialist – extra-European – one.

Even in the extra-European field she often found herself in trouble. It is important to be aware of her struggles and setbacks in this area and period, as well as her 'successes'. The American War of Independence was obviously one, though it can be argued that she only fought that half-heartedly; certainly the American revolutionary cause had as many supporters in contemporary Britain as it had enemies. The Indian 'Mutiny' of 1857–8 – called that, rather than a rebellion, which is what it really was, in order to diminish it – came as a shock, and took the 'might' of the British Empire eighteen months to put down. Even some of the smaller colonial fry proved surprisingly difficult to deal with: the Afghans, for example, whom the British never managed to beat properly; and the Zulus, who inflicted a couple of bloody defeats on them – Isandhlwana the worst one, with 1,329 British soldiers killed – in the 1870s. There were a number of reasons for this. The first was that British technical superiority over Africans and Asians was never as great as it is sometimes assumed to have been; nothing like as overwhelming, for example, as America's military dominance over weak enemies like Iraq and Afghanistan today. The Gatling gun – which only came in in the later 1870s – was not always sufficient to compensate for other disadvantages. These included difficult fighting terrain; long supply lines; vulnerability to local diseases (the obverse of the natives' susceptibility to European ones); small numbers, compared with the huge native armies that could be mustered against them; and poor morale and generally poor human *quality*, among both officers and men, who did not usually represent the pick of their respective social classes in Britain, by contrast with the generally fine generalship, greater courage and infinitely superior motivation of (say) African armies who were defending their own. Even at its height – which most imperial historians place in the mid to late nineteenth century, no later – the Empire was vulnerable. One coordinated push, from within or without, and it could have collapsed.

It wasn't pushed, or at least not then; but the auguries at the turn of the twentieth century genuinely didn't look good. Before about the 1880s two circumstances had run in Britain's favour: firstly, the lack of interest shown by most other European (and American) powers in competing with Britain for overseas colonies, apart from France (most were too taken up with their own internal problems, and content to let the Royal Navy tame their customers for them – the advantage of free trade); and secondly, the ready availability of 'empty' territory for any potential rivals to expand into, should they so wish, without rubbing up against Britain. That was one of the joys of the wider world: there was so much of it. This meant that before the later nineteenth century a 'weak' Britain really only had the Africans and Asians (and an occasional French irritant) to cope with. Then, however, came an important shift. From the 1880s onwards other European powers (and even America) suddenly changed their stance on colonies, and began competing with Britain and France for territory that was now beginning to run short. This coincided with the *perception*, at any rate, that European industry was running short of markets, which therefore needed to be secured abroad in the form of new colonies. A British Royal Commission report of 1886 into the 'Great Depression' of the period (actually the word 'Great' was an exaggeration) made just this point; though this should not necessarily be taken as authoritative, as *liberal* capitalists boycotted it. Clearly this whole situation was worrying for Britain. It was highlighted by the next major conflict featuring the Empire, the South African War of 1899–1902, which Britain won in the end, but only after making a terrible pig's ear of it: with 120,000 British soldiers taking two and a half years to subdue two small republics of Afrikaner (Dutch origin) peasants whose total white *populations* were less than this; raising widespread concerns over how Britain was likely to fare in any future war against a really serious enemy. It was this above everything – more than the 'anti-imperialism' that we have seen the war also provoked – that halted Britain's territorial expansion after 1902. She had reached, or come very near, what Paul Kennedy has called a state of 'imperial overstretch'.

That kept many turn-of-the-century imperialists awake at night. Not a lot of people know this. Here for example is William Pfaff, in his book *Barbarian Sentiments: America in the New Century*:

> Responsible political and economic scholars in 1900 would undoubtedly have described the twentieth-century prospect as continuing imperial rivalries within a Europe-dominated world, lasting paternalistic tutelage by Europeans of their Asian and African colonies . . . etc. All would have been wrong.

Well, it so happens (as Pfaff could have found out himself if he were not so convinced of the differences between the two situations, and had bothered to look) that many turn-of-the-century 'political and economic scholars' *did* address this question; did *not*, in general, predict the continuance of European imperialisms; and so were *not*, in fact, wrong. Most warned of the possibility, even likelihood, that the British Empire would collapse. Several believed *European* imperialism generally was living on borrowed time: threatened by the rise of Russia and America, for example, of Islam, and of China in the slightly longer run. No one was complacent. Many were highly pessimistic.

It was this that motivated the massive propaganda campaign that was set in motion in Britain then to make the Empire more popular among people *they* felt were careless of it, even if our postcolonial theorists can't see this; and was responsible for a number of other quite drastic proposed changes to strengthen the Empire on its home base. These included protectionism: with a vigorous new 'tariff reform' movement starting up in the 1880s, rejecting the old 'free trade' shibboleth utterly, and with half the ruling Conservative Party taking it up in the early 1900s, linking it directly to imperialism through the notion of an 'Imperial *Zollverein*' (or tariff-girt free trade area). There was a great right-wing moral panic at this time over what was called 'national deterioration'; a catch-all phrase that took in physical and mental deficiencies, the enervating effects of peace and ease, certain sexual preferences (masturbation, the 'Oscar Wilde tendency'), the degeneration of the racial 'stock' through Jewish immigration, and football crowds (*sic*): all of which were supposed to be on the increase around the turn of the twentieth century (though how they could tell with masturbation is anyone's guess), ominously for the future of the Empire. New laws against homosexuality and alien immigration were two results of this. Many imperialists also turned against democracy, which they felt was weakening the Empire; and just about all of them opposed women's suffrage, which would 'feminise' it. (Also, how would the Empire's Muslim subjects feel about being legislated for by women?) Military conscription was another suggestion. This was the sort of thing, they felt, that was needed to preserve the Empire in these new, perilous times. Although this is a clearly anachronistic reference, there are signs of a kind of 'proto-fascism' in all this. That, incidentally, was one of Hobson's main arguments against imperialism: its possible repercussions on liberalism at home – what we might call the 'Empire strikes back' effect. The trouble, from the imperialists' point of view – the good news from Hobson's – was that these proposed measures all offended against more powerful national prejudices than the (relatively weak) pro-empire one. It wasn't just a question of showing more 'will', as some right-wingers opined. To adopt all or any of these measures, liberal Britain would have had to fundamentally alter her DNA. As a result, with the possible exception of the opposition to women's suffrage (this was only just defeated in the early 1910s, so the imperial argument against it may have tipped the balance), they mostly failed. Britain never turned into a genuinely imperialist society. As a result, the Empire remained fragile from then on.

As things turned out initially, the imperialists probably needn't have worried too much. There was much huffing and puffing from her new rivals, but never any serious threat. All colonial disputes between them were settled peacefully. The Berlin Conference of 1884–5, called in order to settle European boundaries in west-central Africa, which is often seen as a desperate diplomatic struggle on the part of the powers to grab as much of Africa as they could, was in fact conducted perfectly amicably, partly because no one wanted to provoke a serious war over what to most of them seemed a relatively trivial matter. Gladstone was happy for Bismarck to have as many colonies as he wanted, so long as they did not encroach on Britain's. 'If Germany is to become a colonizing power,' he declared in 1884, 'all I say is "God speed her!" She becomes our ally and partner in the execution of the great purposes of Providence for the advantage of mankind.' Bismarck actually encouraged France's imperial ambitions, in order to take her mind off her defeat by Germany in 1871. At Berlin the pick of the region, the vast

Congo basin, was meekly surrendered to King Leopold of the Belgians (him personally), in order to avoid any sort of a squabble over it among his seniors. A little later Britain actively helped Germany grab a great chunk of East Africa. Thereafter, whenever there seemed a likelihood of a clash – when the frontiers of two expanding European empires bumped into each other, for example – it was *always* settled easily. Wilhelm II's threat in 1896 to challenge Britain in southern Africa (the 'Kaiser's telegram' affair) turned out to be a bluff. When Kitchener (Britain) and Marchand (France) met with their armies at Fashoda on the Nile in September 1898, instead of fighting, they broke open a bottle of champagne between them and waited for their respective Foreign Offices to sort it out. Later Britain and France settled all remaining colonial differences between them in their famous 'Entente' of 1904. A similar agreement followed with Russia three years later. There were no clashes over China (except with the Chinese, of course). Some historians think (or used to) that colonial rivalries lay at the bottom of the outbreak of the First World War in 1914; but it is unlikely that this was so in any obvious and direct way. On the eve of war Britain was quite prepared to satisfy the Germans colonially, albeit at the expense of the Portuguese, whose grip over their colonies was supposed to be slipping (how wrong they were!), rather than of herself. This was still a relatively cheapskate empire. It did not require very much 'power' to lie behind it, and was not itself a sign of British 'power', in most senses of the word – for example, militarily.

The rot set in a little later. After the First World War the illusion of British political power almost collapsed. Indeed, this had been widely predicted before the war, which is why it is ludicrous to think that Britain (apart perhaps from a few imperialist extremists) could possibly have *sought* war with Germany in 1914 – she had far more to lose colonially than to gain. (This does not necessarily absolve her from all responsibility for the war, however. Her empire might be said to have provoked Germany into seeking war, by its very existence. Her navy, which Britain regarded as essential for the defence of her empire, was certainly what triggered Germany's naval expansion, which was undoubtedly a contributory cause of the war.) There was already growing trouble in parts of the Empire in the years immediately preceding 1914: especially in Ireland, India and Egypt. Obviously the main danger of a European war came from the possibility of Britain's defeat by Germany, when presumably many if not all of her colonies would pass to the latter. That didn't happen. But the war gave rise to more crises in the Empire nonetheless. In the upshot Britain did not lose a single colony as a direct result of the fighting, and indeed gained a number, as spoils of her victory. These included most of the old German possessions in Africa and the Pacific (some of them sublet to South Africa and Australia), and a great swathe of the Middle East, connecting Egypt with India, taken from Germany's ally the Ottoman Empire. These weren't officially called 'colonies', but 'mandates' – looked after by Britain on behalf of the new League of Nations; but there was little difference in reality. (We shall return to this in Chapter 2.) This is what made it look as if the British Empire was still on the up in the later 1910s.

But that was an entirely false impression. For a start, the war had clearly weakened it. India had been especially trouble- some, leading to concessions to her nationalists (the 'Montagu–Chelmsford reforms') in 1918, extended later in response to Mahatma Gandhi's brave and skilful campaign. In Ireland the famous 'Easter Rising' of 1916 led (indirectly) to the granting of 'home rule' to most of the island in 1921. That was Britain's earliest and nearest colony – by some ways of looking at it – gone. Egypt had to be given a form of self-government in 1922, albeit with Britain keeping control of the Suez Canal. The mainly loyal 'white' dominions gained a new sense of self- confident independence, resulting in their being conceded control of their own foreign policies after the war. Never again would they be herded into a war simply on the King of England's say-so, as had happened in 1914. (This became significant later.) For 'native' troops employed in the war, it gave them a new sense of their masters' vulnerability, which could be ominous. At home, Britain was close to being impoverished by the war, with her national debt increasing tenfold, for example, which weakened her abroad too. Worse: the war, and the Russian Revolution that happened under cover of it, greatly stimulated socialism in Britain, leading to all kinds of industrial trouble, like the General Strike (1926), and the election of her first ever – albeit a minority – Labour government in 1924. That was particularly worrying for imperialists, imperialism being regarded as a mainly Conservative cause at this time.

Britain's new gains hardly compensated for this. Mesopotamia (Iraq) and Palestine in particular were always more trouble than they were worth (and Iraq's oil was worth quite a lot). In Palestine the problems largely arose from the fact that Britain had promised it (ambiguously) to two different sets of people simultaneously, to secure their help in the war: the Arabs who lived there, and Jews from elsewhere who wanted to 'return'. It was a thankless, draining and in the end hopeless task trying to keep them both apart. Iraq was similarly recalcitrant; and, as well as this, stirred up resentment among British soldiers who had expected to be demobilised when they had done their bit in the 'real' war, rather than be kept on to police foreigners (some even mutinied), and also among middle-class British voters, who jibbed at the taxes they were being asked to bear to pay for this. As a consequence, in 1921 Britain ceased governing Iraq properly, and gave her over to a local emir to rule, so long as he let British companies keep the oil wells and accepted some British troops on his soil. Another malleable emir was found to head 'Transjordan', a new country carved out between Palestine and Iraq. Persia (Iran), the final link in the chain between Egypt and

India, was left for the Iranians and Russians to fight over. The clear reason for all these withdrawals was military weakness, compounded by the British people's reluctance to put themselves out to maintain British control. 'Our small army is far too scattered,' minuted the Chief of the Imperial General Staff in the midst of all this (May 1920). 'In no single theatre are we strong enough – not in Ireland, nor England, not on the Rhine, not in Constantinople, nor Batoum, nor Egypt, nor Palestine, nor Mesopotamia, nor Persia, nor India.' As a result, the great imperial swelling of 1918 went down almost immediately. But it is surprising in many ways that it did not burst. Paul Kennedy has suggested, pertinently, that instead of endlessly analysing why the British Empire 'declined and fell' after the Second World War, we should be asking how it held up so long before then. That's the puzzle.

Borrowed time

So: how *did* it manage it? One way, as we have seen, was through luck. For all of the period before 1914, none of Britain's main imperial rivals made a serious effort to topple her, and the frequent nationalist rebellions that went on never joined up. This continued, almost miraculously, after 1918. Then Britain's major ex- and potential rivals fled the scene. Germany – the main one – was obviously incapable of mounting a challenge for many years after her defeat. Even when she recovered militarily under Hitler, she may not have posed a danger any more to Britain's *empire*: Hitler sometimes hinted that he was perfectly happy for her to carry on with this (he was terribly impressed, by the way, with British rule in India), if Britain would let him have the continent of Europe. (Of course, you did not have to believe him.) France was similarly exhausted. Russia descended into anarchy after her revolution, and then was distracted by her new, radical social experiment at home. The USA – who probably could have mounted a challenge if she had wanted to – withdrew into isolationism, for good liberal and capitalistic reasons, as it seemed to her. She did not even take any part in the postwar League of Nations that might have been an agency for challenging Britain's imperialism, though she had been instrumental in setting it up. Britain was left, then, the only large Western nation with her head above the diplomatic waves of the day, despite the wounds she had sustained under the waterline. For a few years following the end of the war she was virtually the only 'great power' in the world – the only active one, at any rate; but mainly by default, and on borrowed time.

A second factor was bluff. We have alluded to this already: all those fine uniforms and governors' mansions, and the rest of the paraphernalia of British rule, which were supposed to impress the natives with a power that was not really there. In those colonies or parts of colonies that lay near oceans, the Royal Navy gave a much more solid impression of British strength, which this time *was* justified: the Navy was a different kettle of fish from the Army, being genuinely superior to all its rivals. The Navy's main roles in taking or policing colonies were to defeat local navies, if the natives had any (very few did); transport soldiers; and bombard coastlines. The latter can be compared with present-day aerial bombing, with the same drawbacks (mainly, its indiscriminate nature), and the further one, that the Navy's shells could only penetrate a very short distance inland. Still, all those battleships were impressive. A comment by a Brigadier-General in India around 1920 is telling in this connection: British authority was built on 'prestige', he said; once you destroy that, 'the Empire will collapse like a house of cards'. 'Prestige' is – surely – just another name for 'bluff'.

A third way Britain held on was by repression. There are dozens of instances of that throughout her imperial history. The Indian Mutiny and the Jamaica rebellion (1865) had been followed by some terrible reprisals, for example: mass executions, mutineers being 'blown from guns', and so on. The Battle of Omdurman in the Sudan (1898) was a particularly – and, most contemporaries believed, gratuitously – bloody affair. The South African War saw some notorious 'methods of barbarism' employed by British troops, including wholesale farm-burning, and the herding of Boer women and children into 'concentration camps'. (It is unfortunate that the latter phrase has taken on such horrific associations subsequently; the British of course did not set out to exterminate the Boers in this way, but the South African camps were pretty grim places nonetheless – hotbeds of disease.) Alien rule, whatever its other benefits *might* be, invariably gives rise to this sort of thing. We should remember that before wishing it on people today. The years immediately after the First World War saw even worse. Probably the most serious atrocity – certainly the most infamous – was the Amritsar massacre of 1919 in India, when General Reginald Dyer ordered his (Indian) troops to fire into a peaceful meeting of unarmed demonstrators in a square, and to continue firing into their backs as they scrambled to escape, leaving nearly 400 (or it may have been even more) dead. Others were the activities of the notorious 'Black and Tans' – irregular police – in Ireland, and the bombing of suspected rebels from airplanes in Palestine and Iraq. (In the early 1920s that was considered more 'atrocious' than it is today. Several pilots baulked at it.) Thirty years later there were horrific atrocities in colonial Kenya during Britain's last days there, with over a thousand hangings, many of quite innocent people; Africans rounded up into camps surrounded by barbed wire; and tortures of the most obscene kind. This kind of thing didn't entirely stop with the end of overseas empire; there were some nasty things done by the British Army and secret services to Northern Irish rebels in the 1970s, too. Most of these reactions, incidentally, were the results either of fear (Amritsar: Dyer thought another Indian Mutiny was about to start), or of weakness (Iraq: bomber aircraft were a way of keeping order without needing a large army); as well as, in most cases, contempt for the peoples being 'policed' in these ways. They are obviously not an indication of Britain's imperial strength or confidence, except, probably, *vis-à-vis* the poor wretches she was shooting, bombing and torturing. It is arguable that if she had been more powerful, Britain would not have needed to do these atrocious things. On the other hand, she might have found other excuses.

The problems with these 'atrocities' from a British point of view were, firstly, the hatred they engendered among their victims, as is usually the way; and secondly, the disquiet they gave rise to back home. For the British at this time were not generally an atrocious people; or not more so, probably, than anyone else. They usually resiled against reports of such excesses from the colonies. It was the Leader of the Liberal Opposition, later Prime Minister, who coined the phrase 'methods of barbarism' for the Boer War brutalities, for example, not some marginal figure; and the news of Amritsar was greeted with a widespread wave of disgust in the British press, as well as a vigorous defence of Dyer by the old buffers of the day – mostly in the House of Lords. (They tended to be more defensive the more lordly they were.) If it had been left to them this probably wouldn't have mattered; but it was the other classes of Britain, of course, who had the final say on how the Empire was run, at least in constitutional theory. Most didn't have the stomach for this kind of thing. They could digest the Empire, just, albeit with little special taste for it; but not with unpalatable lumps like this in it. This, incidentally, is where Gandhi's genius comes in, in appealing deliberately to the Britons' 'better' side. That of course was a huge compliment to the latter, more no doubt than many of them deserved – Dyer's champions, for example – but not the majority of those who mattered. Gandhi had spotted where the fundamental contradiction of the British Empire lay.

Repression therefore wasn't the complete answer. That left just one more trick. The main way Britain coped with these challenges to her imperial authority in the nineteenth and twentieth centuries was by *giving in* to them, at least to some extent. It can be called 'appeasement', and is a sensible policy in many situations, especially by comparison with repression. There were two varieties of it. The first was to *appear* to give in, but to retain essential control indirectly. The second was to really give in, but retain the appearance of some kind of control in order to save face. There are dozens of examples of both kinds in British imperial history. Gladstone was a master of it. 'Home rule' for Ireland was intended to be the first kind of appeasement, though it failed in his lifetime, and when it eventually succeeded (1921) was more like the second sort. The limited independence he granted to the Transvaal Republic after the First Boer War (1881) was another. The Montagu–Chelmsford package in India (1918) was a third. In the post-First World War Middle East, where Britain found it impossible to rule directly, Arthur Balfour described the first sort of appeasement neatly as 'supreme economic and political control, to be exercised . . . in friendly and unostentatious cooperation with the Arabs, but nevertheless, in the last resort to be exercised'. That – the cooperation of the Arabs – lightened the burden (for Britain). Even in the colonies she ran more directly she deferred to native feelings and customs in very many areas, as we shall see shortly when we come on to British imperial 'rule'. It was the only way she could hang on, with so few personnel on the ground.

This gentler policy also reconciled the Empire to the majority of the British people: adapted it – in appearance, at any rate – to their sensitive stomachs. This became particularly necessary after the First World War, partly because of the widespread attribution of that conflict to the more aggressive sort of imperialism, and the powerful strain of 'internationalist' feeling that grew from this, culminating (at the diplomatic level) in the formation of the

League of Nations. Even the formerly ultra-imperialist Lord
Baden-Powell's Boy Scout movement took this on. Imperialism
– in the old, conventional sense – suddenly became unfashionable. We can tell this from the books about the Empire that were
published in this period, most of the older-fashioned of which
seemed to be on the defensive, while the more 'modern' ones
took an entirely different line on it from before: hugely down-
playing the glorious military aspects of it; almost giving the
impression that most colonies had *asked* to join the Empire;
stressing Britain's supposed 'civilising mission'; and presenting
the whole thing as simply a happy federation of countries at
different stages of 'development'. On South Africa, for example,
the war was skated over, and more was made of Britain's magna-
nimity to the Boers (granting them self-government within the
Empire) afterwards. A new word was coined for it, which was
thought to express this sort of thing better: 'Commonwealth'. A
popular metaphor was that of the 'family'. One or two writers
directly compared it to the League of Nations, which was a clever
ploy if 'internationalists' were to be persuaded on board. This is
quite a change. Much of it was bullshit (not all). But it was
thought to be necessary, if the Empire was to survive *at home.*

Britain's endemic imperial weakness became plain for
everyone to see just before and then just after the Second World
War. Before the war it was clearly one of the reasons for Britain's
most notorious bout of 'appeasement', when it was Hitler who
was appeased, to the perpetual ignominy of those responsible for
it; many of whom, incidentally, were Conservative imperialists,
who believed – correctly, as it turned out – that another
European war would almost certainly spell the end for the
British Empire. (There is also a more direct connection between
the Empire and appeasement. The Dominions – which now
made their own foreign policies, remember – made it plain that
they would not back Britain if she went to war with Germany
over Czechoslovakia in 1938. That was one of the things holding

her back.) Despite this, Britain did declare war on Germany a year later, to make up for the shame of her brief period of appeasement earlier; and landed up on the winning side. Her leader for most of its duration, of course, was Winston Churchill, who, ironically, was one of the keenest imperialists in the Conservative Party. Obviously he didn't see what the other Conservative imperialists saw. He appears to have been one of those fooled by all the interwar propaganda into believing that Britain's colonies loved her too much to be tempted by a war to leave the Empire. 'I have not become the King's First Minister', he famously proclaimed in 1942, 'in order to preside over the liquidation of the British Empire.' Much to his chagrin, he later found he had.

To be fair to Churchill, almost no one predicted the *speed* of Britain's decolonisation after the war; not even the Americans, who were (initially) pushing for it. It mostly happened in the space of about twenty years from 1947 (when Attlee's Labour government appeased the nationalists in the Indian subcontinent), leaving only Rhodesia and Hong Kong as significant remnants after 1970. (Oh, and the Falklands. But no one regarded them as significant before the Argentine attack of 1982 raised their profile somewhat.) It might have happened even more quickly – all the conditions were there for a catastrophic collapse – but for an unexpected American boost for the Empire in the late 1940s and early 1950s, of which more in Chapter 2. On the British side there were a number of imperialists who thought the Empire could be kept going, or even – afterwards – revived. This was the cause espoused by the tiny 'League of Empire Loyalists', for example. (They later merged with the neofascist British National Party.) There is a story – which may be apocryphal – that Enoch Powell, then a young Tory MP and a keen imperialist, burst into Winston Churchill's office just after he had won the 1951 election, offering to reconquer India for the Empire if he would give him ten Army divisions. A number of

other Conservatives thought they could hang on to *some* of the
Empire: mainly the white settlement colonies of south-central
Africa. Others were encouraged by the accession of most of the
ex-colonies to the British 'Commonwealth', which they saw as a
continuation of the Empire in another, more enlightened form.
For years afterwards many old fogies believed – and wrote to the
Daily Telegraph – that Britain could have held on to her Empire
if her people had shown more 'will'. They were probably right
about the 'will'. But that is not to say that if it had been there, the
Empire could have been saved. For a start there were other, material, factors against it: like the devastating economic effects of the
Second World War on Britain, and America's and Russia's
hostility to it (of which more in a later chapter). Secondly, the
forging of an imperial 'will' involved far more than just stiffening
people's sinews. It would have required a social revolution. That
was inconceivable. So the Empire was bound to 'fall'. It was
pre-programmed to.

What did the Empire do for them?

That, in a very small nutshell, is what the British Empire was.
Now (finally) we must turn to what it did. This is more complicated than it is sometimes taken to be. We know what the British
originally wanted to do with their empire, of course. That was to
'exploit' it. That word may have an unpleasant ring to some
people, implying as it does a measure of subjection and immoral
profiteering; but it does not need to carry that baggage. Literally,
'exploitation' simply means 'making use of a resource' (*Oxford
English Dictionary*), and can be done to the benefit of others as
well as of the 'exploiter'. That was how the Victorian British
regarded their own commerce, investment and industrial development in the wider world, especially after it was made 'free'.
(American 'business' is widely seen in a similar way today.)
Colonies could be an aid to that, as a last resort. Very few early or

mid Victorians regarded them in any other light than this; though there were a few missionaries who professed to believe that India, for example, had been given to Britain by God (otherwise how had Britain conquered the former so easily?) in order to bring her to Christ. The main modification to this 'exploitation' motive came when Britons went out to actually *govern* these possessions that their compatriots' commercial enterprise had acquired for them. These men had subtly different notions about what was 'good' for other peoples than either the capitalists or the missionaries; which was what mainly complicates our picture of the 'effects' of the Empire on its subjects. Beyond that, however, there is also the consideration that these people – the governors – weren't allowed to *have* the effect on their wards they would have liked, due to the paucity of their numbers, the more general weakness of the Empire's authority, and official lethargy. That, in fact, was the major factor determining Britain's imperial legacy to her ex-colonies in the twentieth century; in so far as we can disentangle that legacy from 'what would have happened anyway', which is always a problem, of course, with this kind of historical issue.

Some forms of 'capitalist exploitation' are obviously not good for the exploitees. Slavery is the prime example, as most free traders acknowledged; even though some of them may have been a little too sanguine about the benefits that would automatically flow to ex-British slaves when they were liberated into the 'market' after 1834. After then, forms of 'indentured labour' were practised in certain parts of the Empire that came close to formal slavery. That is more problematical, of course; after all, most of the labourers will have signed their own indentures, presumably freely. There were constant rows about this sort of thing in Britain, most famously over the issue of 'Chinese slavery' in South Africa after the Boer War. The most damaging kind of capitalist enterprise in the Empire, however, was the 'settler' kind. We have mentioned settlers already, mainly in an idealistic kind of way: as brave, enterprising, individualistic pioneers. This is why they have founded many of the world's most prosperous and vibrant democracies (including the USA). But there was also another side to them.

In fact, settlers are well known to be some of the most problematical of colonists: the most avaricious, and, in particular, the most careless of other peoples' human and economic rights. The traces of their crimes can be seen all over. It was Australian settlers who perpetrated the worst massacres of their aborigines, for example. The same is true of both colonial and postcolonial North America. It is settlers who, generally speaking, are the most *racist* of imperialists; usually arising from their need (as they perceive it) for land and labour, which predisposes them to believe that the people that have the land and labour they covet are inferior. (We shall return to the general question of racism later.) Settlers were the bane of the Empire, at every stage of its history. Churchill once called the settlers of Natal 'the hooligans of the British Empire'. Kenya, of course, where some of the worst British atrocities took place in the 1950s, was a settler colony (and an upper-class one, to boot). This seems to be a feature of human settlement generally, in areas where there are other less 'advanced' humans living. It is not only a British trait (though the peculiar nastiness of the white Kenyans may have been).

This raises an interesting question about the impact and the morality of imperialism more generally. Most of these phenomena were not the direct responsibility of the British government, which usually professed a duty of 'trusteeship' towards 'natives', and in some cases tried (if not very strenuously) to hold the settlers back. An example of this may be America in the later eighteenth century; where it can be argued that one of the motives for local settler resentment against the British connection (together with the better known tea tax) was their desire to continue their expropriation and elimination (even genocide) of the native peoples to the west of the original thirteen colonies, against the wishes of the imperial government – the latter objecting on both practical and moral grounds. Both these positions can be seen as 'imperialistic', but pulling in opposite directions. The settlers were certainly behaving 'imperialistically' in most senses, despite their paper status as Britain's imperial 'subjects'. Another example is the struggle at the beginning of the nineteenth century between plantation owners and humanitarians in the West Indies over the issue of slavery. (Jane Austen's *Mansfield Park* hints at this, for careful readers.) Both these groups were also 'imperialist', of course, but their imperialism meant very different things to them. In the case of the plantation owners it gave them the right to keep slaves. For the humanitarians, it conferred on them the *duty* to liberate them. In this case the latter kind of imperialist won out eventually. In most cases of 'settlement', however, they didn't. They can be criticised for that, of course – for not trying harder.

What these horrors cannot be blamed on, however, is 'imperialism' *per se*. Indeed, it is arguable that the best corrective to them, at that time in history, would have been *more* imperialism (of the metropolitan sort). That might have saved many of the 'Indians' of the great American plains, for example; as well as – as we have seen – giving Afro-Americans another thirty years of liberty. On the other hand, Britain might not have bothered. She was short of resources, after all. And the fact that Australia still had colonial status throughout the nineteenth century didn't do her aborigines much good. The *theoretical* issue, however, is a genuine one. Later on it lay behind some socialists' preference for imperialism of a sort (a very social-democratic sort), over what they regarded as the potentially more tyrannous *effective* imperialism of the free market (or 'globalisation'). Even J. A. Hobson, the doyen of twentieth-century anti-imperialists, agreed that it was possible to envision situations in which 'imperialism' was preferable to 'freedom', on 'libertarian' grounds. Theoretically.

That was also the position taken by most British imperialists in the nineteenth and early twentieth centuries – practically. Certain peoples were self-evidently 'free-er' under British rule than left to their own devices. 'Free' of course did not mean 'democratic' then: for most of this period Britain did not have that for her own people, though she considered herself a 'free' country; rather it signified things like individual rights, security against arbitrary government, liberty of conscience, peace, the right to regulate your own affairs generally, and (this was the clincher for capitalists) the right to buy and sell – goods, land, labour, whatever. These were what British government was supposed to bring with it, and what were thought to make British imperialism distinctive from other kinds (though it probably wasn't).

One example is worth elaborating briefly, if only because it is sometimes used as a precedent – a cautionary one – for certain modern American foreign policy adventures: Britain's *de facto* rule over Egypt after 1882. Egypt had been invaded originally – by the self-styled anti-imperialist Gladstone – in order to 'liberate' the country from the corrupt and tyrannical administration of a local khedive who had plunged the place into ruinous debt. He was replaced – effectively; formally Egypt was still supposed to be independent – by a British 'Resident' who just happened to be a scion of a famous banking family (the Barings), and who saw his main task thereafter as restoring Egypt's finances, as the essential – and only necessary – means for its future progress, with the help of foreign investment. The reasons this is often compared to the Iraq invasion of 2003 are Gladstone's continued protests that it did not count as 'imperialism' (anticipating Rumsfeld); his insistence that he intended to withdraw his troops from Egypt as soon as she could stand on her own feet; the nationalist reaction the British invasion nonetheless provoked, which rendered this impossible; and suspicions of more nefarious motives underneath. (Gladstone held Egyptian bonds.) There was also a Muslim fundamentalist leader hovering in the background, the 'Mahdi' (Muhammed Ahmad), who gave much trouble over the next fifteen years. Superficially the resemblances do seem rather startling. The main point, however, is that the British government certainly felt that its intervention here, as almost everywhere, was 'liberating'. It would not have been able to face its constituency otherwise.

The ruling class

Egypt, however, was exceptional among British colonies (or 'colonies') in many ways: not least in having a capitalist put in control of her. This wasn't usually how things were done. One reason was that capitalists are, as a general rule, not all that keen on ruling. It doesn't come naturally to them. They tend to be hostile to 'government' generally, which they see mainly as a restraint on enterprise; and, on a personal level, don't find 'ruling' half as worthwhile or satisfying as making money (and so enriching society generally). This is why a terrifically capitalistic power like the USA today is not at all keen on governing newly conquered countries like Afghanistan and Iraq, and is not, it has to be said, very good at it. Capitalists prefer to leave countries 'free'; or, by a more cynical way of looking at it, to dominate or control them in less direct and obvious ways. The positive side of this, and one clear difference between the old British and the new American empires, is the latter's willingness – indeed, almost desperation – to devolve the government of its conquests to democratically elected governments as soon as possible. One negative aspect is that if this cannot be done – if democracy (or a compliant democracy) seems not to be an option – the Americans do not have much to offer in its stead.

Britain did. This was because she was not as terrifically capitalist as America is. By contemporary standards, of course, she was: easily the leading capitalist economy in the world for most if not all of the nineteenth century, and with a society and polity, too, which reflected this. The middle classes for example dominated Parliament after 1832 (the 'Great Reform Bill'), at least indirectly, which is why all that free trade legislation was able to be passed in the 1830s and '40s, initially against aristocratic and country opposition. This however is not the whole story. The middle classes never displaced the upper classes in British society, and least of all in government, which continued to be dominated by upper-class *personnel*. (At least half of all Cabinets were members of the House of Lords as late as the 1900s.) The reason they were there is quite straightforward. They *liked* governing, indeed felt that they were specially born to it, and were groomed for it in their 'public' (i.e. private) schools; which saved the middle classes the trouble. So long as the upper classes did as the middle classes asked – like enacting free trade – that was OK. And by and large they did, generally out of conviction; Lord Palmerston, for example, arguably the greatest Foreign Secretary of the nineteenth century and Prime Minister for nine years, had had 'political economy' knocked into him in his teens by a disciple of Adam Smith, no less. Upper-class government was also supposed to be less prone to corruption than middle-class government, which was probably the case. There was a strong convention that ministers should not profit in any material way from their positions (apart from their salaries, of course). That was carried over into the colonial field. British administrators abroad were not allowed to own property or have business interests there. That was probably another factor putting the capitalists off.

It was to these other men therefore that Britain turned when she needed governors, district officers and the like to rule the territories that her material interests (capitalism) had accrued for her. This immediately introduced a certain incongruity into the situation, even a contradiction; for these men did not by and large share the values of the capitalist classes – indeed, were usually taught to despise them in their schools – and consequently were unlikely in the colonies, far from the immediate control of their British middle-class masters, to rule their new subjects in an entirely capitalist way. Sometimes they actively obstructed the capitalists, who often complained of this, for example in India. More often their priorities were simply different. The British ruling classes were generally conservative; less zealous about liberalism or free trade or Christianity – or anything else (apart from various ways of killing animals for sport) – than the British middle classes tended to be; more respectful of the age-old customs they met in many of the colonies they came to run, partly because they reminded them of their own (hierarchy, what David Cannadine calls 'ornamentalism', or dressing up, and so on); and from a strictly practical point of view nervous of the sorts of liberal 'reforms' that the middle classes favoured, but which were likely to unsettle their 'natives', and consequently make them more difficult to control. For these men were, it will be recalled – it is almost the most important thing we need to remember about them – a very small *number*, relative to the hundreds of millions of people they were supposed to rule: around 2,000 in India in the 1890s, and not many more in the whole of the remainder of the empire. The reason for this was that their middle-class masters in Britain demanded that the colonies had to be ruled cheaply, if they were to be ruled at all; ideally from their own resources. That did not allow for much administration, if they were poor. A consequence of all this was that Britain's colonial rulers were never really in a position to force radical change, capitalist or otherwise, on anyone. This is one of the reasons – though not the only one – for the general ineffectiveness which is the main overall characteristic of British imperial rule, judged in terms of political development, during most of the nineteenth and early twentieth centuries, despite claims to the contrary from both ends of the imperialist/anti-imperial spectrum: claims that it 'civilised' its subjects, for example, or ruined them.

Not that the attempt wasn't ever made. The early nineteenth century in particular was a time of great hope for the 'improvement' and 'progress' of 'native' peoples all over the world, when it was felt that basically all one needed to do was to show the natives the self-evident superiority of the British way of doing things, in economics, religion, law, politics and just about every other area (except art: the British acknowledged that they were inferior here – indeed, took a certain pride in it), for them to quickly and gratefully fall in line. It should have been easy. It was tried in India, with fundamental land reforms along British lines, increased trade (of course), the abolition of barbaric practices (*sati*, or the burning of widows, is the most notorious example), new forms of justice, English-style education for an elite, and the encouragement of Christian proselytism; all designed, as William Wilberforce, the great anti-slavery leader, put it, 'to strike our roots into the soil by the gradual introduction of our own principles and opinion; of our laws, institutions, and manners; above all, as the source of every other improvement, of our religion, and consequently of our morals', in order to 'raise' the Indians in what was often called 'the scale of civilisation'. Thomas Macaulay, the historian who was also on India's supreme council, saw the ultimate outcome of all this as Indian self-government under a parliamentary system; which, when it was achieved, he thought, would be 'the proudest day in English history'. This was 'nation-building' with a vengeance. Some of it worked. *Sati* was banned. A generation of elite Indians was brought up as English gentlemen, and liberals to boot. Capitalist trade and land ownership gradually spread through the vast subcontinent. Up to the 1850s, the project looked to be going well.

Then, however, came the shock of the 'Mutiny'. Instead of showing gratitude for all these blessings, the Indians – or a large number of them – turned and bit the hand that was blessing them. This was a matter of genuine puzzlement to many Britons; it 'remains mysterious' wrote another liberal historian, J. R. Green, seventeen years after the event. This explains the savagery of Britain's initial repression of the rebellion (the blowing from cannons), and the longer-term hardening of race prejudice to which it may have given rise. People began to wonder whether non-Europeans *could* be 'civilised'. There were also, however, kinder ways of analysing it. Benjamin Disraeli, for example, blamed the Mutiny on British arrogance; in particular, a liberal lack of respect for other cultures. (He obviously had in mind here English Tory culture, too.) Another imperialist, Alfred Lyall, had a more general explanation. 'I know of no instance in history', he wrote in 1882, 'of a nation being educated by another nation into self-government and independence; every nation has fought its way up the world as the English have done.' That knocks 'nation-building' right on the head. And of course it is what happened with India (and Pakistan) ultimately.

In the meantime, however, Britain's 'civilising mission' had had the wind taken out of its sails more than a little. British imperialists never stopped talking about it, and maybe genuinely believing it: it was one of their main justifications for empire, after all, especially for those who did not feel entirely comfortable with its commercial (or 'mercenary') rationale; but they appeared less sanguine. That lack of Indian gratitude hurt. Later, in a famous poem Kipling wrote to persuade the Americans to share what he called the 'white man's burden' with Britain, this appeared as one of the 'burden's' inevitable corollaries for those who took it up: 'The blame of those ye better,/ The hate of those ye guard.' For him, this was one of its heroic aspects: how much nobler to do good to people *without* their thanking you! But it made 'civilising' a somewhat grim, stoical task. It also looked like taking longer than had been hoped originally. As the nineteenth century wore on, the time-line stretched out. One common way of measuring it was by looking at how long it had taken the Europeans to progress from, say, barbarity to civilisation, or feudalism to liberalism, and apply that to the Africans, Indians, or whomever. 'It took *us* five hundred (or a thousand, or two thousand) years,' was a frequent argument; 'why should we expect these others to do it in less?' One good thing about this was that it assumed that all peoples were *capable* of progress: so it wasn't, strictly speaking, a racist view; but it obviously was not likely to encourage imperialists to try to hurry it on. This was another dampener on the 'civilising mission' aspect of British imperialism; together with the simple problem of resources (the small numbers of District Officers, and the rest) that has already been mentioned.

For many this was probably just an excuse. They paid lip-service to the idea of colonial 'progress', and even ultimate self-government, but only because they thought it would not come in their time. Some believed quite frankly that British imperial control over many of these peoples would always be required, simply because they would never be capable of ruling themselves. Belief in the *irremediable* inferiority of other races was fairly widespread among many of the imperial class in nine-teenth- and twentieth-century Britain, though not quite as ubiquitous as is sometimes assumed. (The influence of certain Victorian intellectuals has been greatly exaggerated.) It was undoubtedly boosted by the excesses of the Indian Mutiny, and certain other bloody colonial events that came soon afterwards: Maori atrocities in New Zealand, for example, and black barbarities during the Jamaica rebellion of 1865; or, rather, by the selection of these (isolated) events for opprobrium by newspapers and others, in preference to the equally atrocious actions of Europeans, in a way that implied – as it was meant to – that atrocity was a uniquely non-European trait. If colonial subjects were biologically inferior, then trying to 'civilise' them was obviously pointless. Policing and caring for them was about all one could do. (Some, of course, inferred more chilling lessons from this, but they were not usually colonial administrators.)

There was, however, yet another approach to 'native policy', as it was invariably called in Britain, which rested on a quite distinct assumption from either of these. This was that the 'native' was neither 'improvable' on Western lines, nor 'inferior', but was simply *different*, with customs and cultures which were neither better nor worse than the European, and which deserved to be nurtured, therefore, in their own right. This may surprise those whose image of British imperial rule, even at its best, is of a dominant culture arrogantly trying to force its own ways on everyone else; but it ties in with the values of the class that was actually ruling these places in this period, which were, as we have seen, not necessarily the same as those of the classes in whose interests the colonies were originally taken – not so 'ideological', for example. (We saw a glimpse of this in Disraeli's reaction to the Indian Mutiny.) There is evidence to show that throughout the history of Britain's colonial empire the people she sent out to run it often appreciated what they found there rather more than did the middle classes back home. David Cannadine, for example, has made much of this perceived affinity between feudal Britons and the 'traditional' cultures of Asia and Africa; which may be one of the things – the degree of empathy between them – that enabled the former, despite their small numbers, to maintain their authority for so long: they didn't rub the local hierarchies up as much as the bourgeois would have done. At the beginning of the twentieth century this approach became formalised in a new and distinctively British 'philosophy' of colonial government, called 'indirect rule', or 'rule the native on native lines'; the idea being that instead of 'modernising' whole societies, or even their elites, the British colonial authorities should simply help them to 'progress' in their own, different, ways. One aspect of this was the deliberate preservation of 'peasant proprietorship' in certain colonies (like Nigeria), against the tide of capitalist land ownership that was threatening to engulf them – to the annoyance, of course, of the capitalists. (William Lever, one of them, decamped his enterprises from Nigeria to the Congo in protest.)

We must not exaggerate or over idealise this tendency. It was only implemented in a very few colonies. Where it was implemented, it was as much for practical as for philosophical reasons (again, lack of resources to 'modernise' properly, and the need to avoid stirring up the natives). There are problems with it in any case: was it realistic to try to cushion old ways of doing things from the inevitable impact of the 'modern' world in this fashion? Some of these 'old ways' were only dubiously authentic in any case. The policy was greatly resented by many Africans themselves, especially those who had already undergone some European acculturation, and who read it as an attempt by the Europeans to keep them 'down': which in many ways it undoubtedly was. In any event, however, it was another factor militating against the 'civilising mission' side of British imperialism; which, in truth, was only a very small part of its agenda overall.

Non-officials

This is especially so if one considers *all* the agencies that were involved in it, of which the official colonial authorities – the Colonial and India Offices and their servants – were only one. Others included traders, capitalists, settlers, missionaries, even perhaps explorers and travellers. This in fact was a characteristic feature of British imperialism, marking it out from other empires that have been more tightly in the grips of their metropoles. Britain left far more to private enterprise. We have insisted before that this does not absolve her of blame for the crimes of some of her entrepreneurs – she was, after all, ultimately responsible for them; but she genuinely had only limited practical control over them (like any government over a private company). These people's impact on the way the colonies were effectively run could be considerable – even greater than Whitehall's. Often they pulled against each other. This is another reason why it is so misleading to generalise about British imperial rule. We have met one example already: the planter/humanitarian battle in the early nineteenth century over the issue of slavery. We can find similar disagreements in other colonial situations. In West Africa in the later nineteenth century, for instance, missionaries who wished to 'save' the Africans were constantly clashing with traders, who wanted them left as they were. There were other competing groups and interests here too: like the large-scale capitalists and settlers who saw the Africans mainly in terms of labour; and then, of course, the 'DOs' (District Officers), who were nervous of the social disruption their wholesale proletarianisation might cause.

Each of these approaches involved a different view of 'race'. The tendency among missionaries was to believe that Africans were potentially equal to Europeans, but corrupted by 'superstition' (that is, by different superstitions from theirs). Traders held that they were generally good fellows. Settlers by and large regarded them as fit only to work for the more advanced and efficient white man. Government officers, latterly, saw them as representing different forms of human culture, which should be preserved. Yet again, this undermines the notion that Victorian Britain manifested a consistent *kind*, at least, of 'racism'; and even possibly the idea, common among some modern scholars, that this racism was fundamentally rooted in the culture of the metropole. On the contrary, it seems far more likely that race attitudes derived from or were at least substantially modified by these different groups' *functions* in the colonies when they got out there. Missionaries needed to believe the Africans were improvable if they were to bother trying to improve them, for example; genuinely 'free' traders needed to rub along with them; it was obviously convenient for settlers and plantation owners to believe that their labourers were fit for nothing better; DOs needed to respect 'native' cultures because they had to work through them, and so on. Most British colonies in the nineteenth and early twentieth centuries were riven by disagreements and disputes along these sorts of lines.

Which policy came to dominate in any particular colony depended largely on the local balance of power between these interests. The Colonial Office was often the least powerful. We have already noticed the problems it had in enforcing its authority directly. So it generally ruled through surrogates, at least for some of its functions. Often these were European settlers, in those parts of the Empire that were suited to them. They were a cheap solution for the Colonial Office, and good news for the settlers themselves, but usually disastrous for the *indigènes*. That was even so, as we have seen, where the settlers were upper class and 'public' school educated (as in Kenya): so one couldn't *rely* on *noblesse oblige*. (One contemporary noticed how even some of the best educated public schoolboys tended to 'go bad' in the tropics.) Often the Colonial Office disapproved of what the settlers were doing, and of their attitudes. There was much hand-wringing over this, and some attempts to rein them back. When the new Union of South Africa was formally given over to the whites to rule in 1911, for example, parts of it (Basutoland, Bechuanaland and Swaziland) were reserved to the British government because it did not trust the white South Africans to run them. (It also, incidentally, hoped – probably genuinely – that the latter would grow more racially liberal in time.) In Rhodesia and Kenya it stalled the local whites for decades, never ever granting *formal* political power to them. But it still allowed them considerable leeway, and defended the Kenyan settlers militarily (and atrociously), mainly to make up for its own small numbers of administrative personnel. That was a blatant and culpable dereliction of duty, for a government that always professed to be holding these colonies 'in trust' for their native inhabitants.

Elsewhere the people with power – much of it, at any rate – were European missionaries; doctors; teachers; those capitalists who were still allowed to operate in the colonies (as most were); and local native partners, or 'collaborators'. Collaboration, in fact, was one of the basic building bricks of the British Empire. It can be seen most clearly in British India, about a half of which (in area) was ruled by 'native princes'. This is usually coloured a lighter shade of pink on contemporary maps. The princes were not entirely free agents, of course: they had to govern in ways the British regarded as responsible; but they could still be, for example, as conservative as they liked. Again, this did not exactly conduce to 'progress'. In vaguer ways the same pattern was followed in nearly all of Britain's non-settler colonies, even the deepest dyed red ones; chiefs, emirs, sultans, maharajas, local educated elites, all became effectively Britain's clients there, allowed to retain their positions and privileges, and to block any real political change, in return for saving Britain the trouble of ruling their countries directly. It was cleverly done, in the main. This is what the British upper classes – those that didn't go bad in the tropics – were good at; *not* – emphatically – 'nation-building'.

That's why so few viable nations were built under the British. When colonial independence came, in the 1950s and '60s, many imperialists claimed that it was premature: that they needed another twenty or fifty years to prepare their colonies for self-government properly; forgetting that they had already been given those twenty or fifty years, twenty or fifty years earlier. They had done little with them. The interwar years in particular were a period of stagnation in most parts of the Empire (the 'mothball phase', as one historian of Tanganyika calls it), with minimal economic development, and only a miserly amount of government money granted for it, by a Labour government in

1929; and almost no moves towards any kind of indigenous political progress, except in the case of India, where it was forced on the government by the much more advanced, powerful and angry nationalist movement that was active there. This is not to criticise the men 'in the field' in the colonies necessarily, those famous DOs in their khaki shorts and pith helmets, sweating in the tropical heat; most of whom seem to have been decent enough chaps, and genuinely concerned to do good – according to their lights – for their natives, albeit also rather unimaginative, perhaps – even stupid. (Sir Ralph Furse, who recruited most of the Colonial Office ones, didn't like 'cleverness'.) We don't need to demonise them in order to be critical of British colonial policy in this period generally, which of course was the government's and Whitehall's doing, not theirs. Their excuses were that they didn't *have* the men in the field; that money was tight, after the Great War and then into the Great Depression; and that they thought they had more time for the job than they had. But that does not seem adequate. About the only positive and successful imperial initiative carried out at this time was the achievement at last, in the 1930s, of the earlier generation of imperialists' dream of an imperial tariff union. And that had the negative effect of hugely irritating the Americans when Britain, because of her imperial weakness, needed them most, as we shall see.

For those who are fond of historical precedents, this sets out the British one for modern American 'imperialism'. It may be different from what some readers expected. It will almost certainly be more complex and ambivalent, certainly than most popular versions of the story tell it. There can be no doubt at all about that, even if parts of the foregoing analysis may be biased, or wrong. Readers familiar with recent American foreign policy will have heard some bells ringing as they read this chapter – all those imperial denials, to take perhaps the most surprising example; but also, hopefully, will have been aware of the differences – of relative strengths, ruling ethoses, and ideals. All these are interesting, and may be instructive. We shall be coming on to them again in the next chapter but one. Before this, however, we need to examine some of the indigenous historical roots of American imperialism. That is what Chapter 2 will be about.

2

'Not colonies, but outposts'
The American imperial tradition

Common roots

'Imperialism' has never been one of the things that have differentiated Britain from America. During the twentieth century the myth arose that this was one of the essential contrasts between them. Britain was an old-fashioned conquering and annexing power; America 'the first continental, outward-looking, *non*-imperialist power in history', in the words of Lawrence Summers (he of the 'women can't do math' row when he became President of Harvard later on). But it is not true. Throughout the nineteenth century, and for some way into the twentieth, Britain and America pursued almost identical imperial paths; or, at any rate, paths that can be regarded as 'imperial' in some lights.

We shouldn't be surprised at this. America and Britain were similar countries at the time of their separation, with most of the former's 'liberties', of course, deriving from the latter; and they developed thereafter in rough parallel. In both countries the general trend was towards a broadening out of 'freedom'. This is obvious in America's case, with the abolition of slavery in 1865, for example; the widening of the political franchise both at state and federal levels, to include women nationwide in 1920; and similar advances in religious and economic freedom. But Britain did not stay still either. Much of her development took a similar path, albeit with slight deviations from the American line. She had already long abolished slavery on her own soil, of course, and was to do so in her colonial possessions thirty years before America, as we have seen. On the political front she was slower, but soon caught up with America in male democracy; and gave women the vote nationally a couple of years ahead of her. The persistence of her monarchy gave the impression of reactionism, but that is easily explained. Britain simply solved the 'overmighty king' problem, which had been common to both of them, in a different way – not by replacing him with an elective one, as in America, but by progressively and drastically whittling down his (or her) powers. These were different means to the same basic end. Neither system is obviously 'more' democratic than the other; each has its democratic drawbacks and advantages. Later on both countries flirted with more 'social' (or social*ist*) forms of freedom, but with Britain taking to them slightly more enthusiastically, at least for a time. Nonetheless, the latter's relatively individualist ethos is one of the things that pushes her *closer* to America today, than for example to her European neighbours. Economically she was, if anything, 'free-er' (more capitalist) than the US for most of the time. She invented the industrial revolution, of course. There were some important differences, to be sure. One was Britain's retention of her aristocracy, which America did not have in quite the same form. (Her slaveocracy and plutocracy were comparable, but not identical, and they didn't exactly have a House of Lords.) This, as we have already seen, was crucial in the context of the subject-matter of this book. There were others, too. But these – and superficial appearances, like the flummery surrounding Britain's ridiculous monarchy – should not blind us to the two countries' continuing similarities in most respects. (Actually, modern America can be as flummery as Britain when she likes.) So they were not likely to differ when it came to 'imperialism'.

Only three things obscure this obvious fact. The first is the persistence of the myth of 'exceptionalism' in America – that she is essentially different from other countries in the face of the evidence in the previous paragraph; from which it follows that she *can't* have been imperialist. (We shall return to this in Chapter 3.) The second is a fundamental misunderstanding of the nature of *British* imperialism during this period, which the last chapter tried to sort out. The third is semantics. The problem here is the American insistence that the word 'imperialism' only applies to the *formal* acquisition of territory *overseas*. Even by that definition America has her clear exceptions, as we shall see shortly. By empire deniers these (the Philippines, and so on) are usually explained away as 'aberrations'; but they were only that if you believe in the importance of the 'overseas' thing. This, however, is not a reasonable condition to set, either logically – why should a stretch of water make all that difference? – or historically – look at the Roman Empire. In the 1940s it was known by British imperialists as the 'salt water fallacy'. If we disregard that, then the imperial and imperial*ist* history of the United States right from its beginning is clear-cut. This is well known to most historians of America, but less so to others; so it may be worth spelling out here.

Manifest destiny

The idea of America as an 'anti-imperialist' power, in fact, is a fairly recent construction, and has everything to do with the bad odour that came to surround the word in the early twentieth century. It certainly didn't go back to her origins. Few of the original American revolutionaries were against imperialism in principle; they were just against *Britain's* imperial rule over *them*. One of the grievances they had against that, as we saw, was that it was preventing the westward expansion that many of them hankered after, but that London was more chary of. Once Britain was shaken off, the colonists were free to pursue their own imperial designs. Many even used that word for it: America, wrote an enthusiastic Bostonian in 1789, would probably become in time 'the largest empire that ever existed', covering first the entire north American continent, then the Caribbean islands, and then – who knew? John Quincy Adams predicted her dominating South as well as North America ultimately. On a slightly different tack, George Washington thought that, however insignificant the thirteen States seemed then, there would come a time 'when this country will have some weight in the scale of Empires'. (Many eighteenth-century Britons, incidentally, foresaw the same thing.) 'Empire' could mean many different things at this time, of course, so we should not make the obvious mistake of assuming that when the word was used then it must have carried all its later resonances. It did not. It is clear, however, that many early leading Americans saw their nation as a fundamentally *expansionist* power, right from the beginning; with their expansion not necessarily stopping at the borders of Canada and Mexico, or at the shores of the Pacific. For many of them, in fact, 'expansion' was as important, and as American, as 'liberty'.

Initially, of course, this expansion mainly took place in America's own back yard. Its story is well known: the steady march of the new Americans from east to west, reaching the Mississippi in the 1840s, the Pacific in the 1860s, and then the next forty or so years spent in filling in the spaces between. (Some of them, incidentally, sailed round to California rather than trekking there. It could be easier. So some salt water was involved.) This is not usually called 'imperialism', but the 'opening up of the West', or 'expansion', or some other similar more neutral term. Another justification for this is that the American colonists were 'free' men and women, who soon after they had 'tamed' their new territories were always given self-government as 'States', which is supposed to make them different from British colonists: except that it doesn't, as we have seen.

Australians were just as practically free as Arizonans, except of course their convicts (and America had plenty of those). Then there is the curious idea that the West belonged to the Americans all along *really*, that it was their 'destiny' to take over their whole continent, even a God-given one: which may be so (who can be sure that he or she knows the mind of God?), but is difficult for a rational person to take seriously. One or two religious Britons thought the same of India and Africa: that God had given them to Britain to 'save their souls'; except that in these cases this wasn't meant to deny Britain's 'imperialism' there, but rather to justify it.

Otherwise America's westward expansion displayed many common imperialist features. It was very violent, with war playing a great part in it: indeed, a far greater part in the US's history generally than is often recognised. It disregarded the claims of the existing inhabitants of these territories, claiming that they were '*terrae nullius*' (no one's). That mirrors Britain's expansion into Canada, Australasia and southern Africa. Another similarity is the racism and atrociousness that were involved in both cases. These were, after all, settlers. As well as the natives, the Americans took territory from other European powers (Spain, France, Russia) and from Mexico, either through war, or purchase, or both; which is something Britain by and large did not do between 1815 and 1914. America would have liked to have taken British North America (later Canada) also, but that proved too tough for her. Otherwise her progress across the continent was relatively easy, with the native Americans unable to mount really effective resistances, however bravely they fought, though the whites made as much as they could of the setbacks they did encounter, in order to magnify the supposed 'heroism' of their deeds. Again, the British parallels are glaring. (Little Big Horn, 1876, for example, was America's Isandhlwana, 1879.) A *more* imperialistic feature in America's case was the way the myths surrounding all this later percolated into the cultural consciousness of the whole nation. Britain, by contrast, had no close equivalent of the 'Western' novel, show or movie. By most ways of looking at it this was classic 'imperialism'; one of a piece with Britain's. It is only not, if you insist you have to get there by boat.

The roots of the special dynamism displayed in both these cases are unclear; the most likely source – because it is one the Americans shared with most other contemporary expansionary powers (though possibly not Russia) – was economic: the material needs of the capitalist system, and the ethic that went along with this. (Capitalism is supposed to be characteristically dynamic. Who ever heard of a business aiming for *stability*?) Even before the 1890s this had taken many other Americans overseas (in boats), albeit in less than overtly imperialist ways. The US's overseas trade trebled during the last forty years of the nineteenth century, for example, spreading all over: to Europe and Latin America predominantly, but also – and increasingly – to Asia in the west. Trade is not intrinsically imperialist (at least, not by my definition), and indeed in some circles is regarded, as we saw in the last chapter, as its antithesis or antidote. Ideally it is carried on between equal partners. You choose to sell; I choose to buy. But as we saw in the case of nineteenth-century Britain, it also needs certain conditions to enable it, which may be difficult to achieve outside your own borders, and in so-called 'primitive' countries (of which there were many in the nineteenth century), without an element of coercion from outside. This is what could give rise to an 'imperialism' of sorts, whoever is doing the trading. Later, William Appleman Williams coined the phrase 'open door imperialism' for it. Some radicals see it at the root of 'globalisation' today.

For example: from the 1840s onwards the US had been signing commercial treaties with the Chinese government which could – just like Britain's – be regarded as not entirely free and fair. That she did not need to go further in this was partly due to the work the British Royal Navy had already done in opening up Chinese trade to everyone. The Opium Wars freed things up for American merchants too. America's equivalent were the famous treaties her Admiral Matthew Perry forced on Japan in 1853–4, though on this occasion the mere threat of bombardment was sufficient, and nothing as disreputable as opium, of course, was involved. Again like Britain, America also required secure sea routes for her trade. This led to one or two overseas annexations early on, including several Pacific islands in the 1850s and 1860s, some of which, like the uninhabited Midway atoll, were a good 3,000–4,000 miles distant from the nearest part of mainland America; but, more importantly, it also led to a more subtle policy of staking out 'spheres of influence' in order to signal America's interest in certain regions, and warn rivals off. The Monroe Doctrine, announced in 1823, and covering the entire Americas, marked the beginning of this. In the 1870s the Hawaiian Islands – 2,500 miles away – were added to that. In Hawaii in particular, but also elsewhere, American business interests often took a hold on local economies which was stifling, at best. (In Hawaii it was American sugar growers.) Elsewhere within the 'Monroe' area (Cuba and Panama, for example) there was frequent US interference, either official ('gunboat diplomacy', it would have been called, if it had been Palmerston doing it) or, more often, by private 'filibusterers', in the affairs of other countries. Whether all this amounts to 'imperialism' is really a matter of individual judgement, mainly about semantics. The point is, however, that it is very close indeed – identical in many respects – to many things that Britain was doing at exactly this time, and which are commonly called 'imperialism' in her case.

This is why that sudden shift to a more obvious kind of imperialism in 1897–8 was not really 'aberrant'; it followed on quite logically from what had gone before. Again, we don't need to go into details; in a nutshell, it involved the annexation of Hawaii as a formal colony for the first time, together with the Philippines, Puerto Rico, Guam, part of Samoa, and the tiny Johnston, Palmyra and Wake Islands in the north Pacific, all taken from the Spaniards. In addition, Cuba was taken from them; but then, shortly afterwards, handed over to local people to run. Later on (1903) America added the Panama Canal Zone – hacked out of Colombia – to her haul. That made up a tidy little collection of obvious colonies; on nothing like the scale of Britain's empire, of course, but then America had started later, and had been busy before then, as we have seen, in her own back yard. (Also, she evinced no interest in Africa, where most of the remaining colonisable territory in the very late nineteenth century lay.) No one denies the appellation of 'imperialism' to *this*.

Economic considerations were clearly important here. Indeed, scarcely any Americans denied it, for reasons we shall come on to a little later; so unless they were merely *pretending* to be avaricious, there is little reason to doubt it. The imminent filling up of the 'West' was one reason it happened then. Frederic Jackson Turner's famous 'thesis' (1893), that expansion was the essential feature of American history, implying that it would need to continue in some other way when the last American frontier was reached, elevated this into a grand national philosophy. (Turner was America's J. R. Seeley.) Also important were widespread contemporary concerns about trade. From the 1870s onwards American exports were coming to exceed imports regularly, which was supposed to indicate a worrying 'surplus' of the goods grown or extracted or manufactured at home. During that decade and the following two, recurrent depressions, and the working-class misery that accompanied them, expressed in strikes and socialism, produced the sort of perceived need for foreign markets that could easily lead to demands on governments to apply *pressure* for them. A business journal in 1885, for example, had expressly advocated a 'spirited foreign policy' in order to open up the required markets forcibly. Exactly the same was being pleaded in Britain at the same time, as we saw. This obviously shades into 'economic imperialism'. It is what the Americans got in 1897–8.

There was also an idealistic side to it, however, though not in *opposition* to the mercenary one: which is a special characteristic of American foreign policy, though by no means exclusive to it. Slightly more than in Britain, trade was seen as 'liberation'. Forcing it on others, therefore, was not to challenge their 'freedom' essentially. The exchange of goods between peoples was bound to make them free-er as well as more prosperous, even if they didn't appreciate it at the time. Secondly, it was a way of spreading other American 'values' into the world. This was peculiar to America. Because of the special nature of the USA's origins, the nature of her 'patriotism' (or nationalism), the parochialism of her culture, and *possibly* because it is true, those values were supposed to be universal, valid for everyone: expressed in the rhetoric of 'liberty' and 'freedom' that Americans employed ubiquitously, without, in most cases, any sense of the intrinsically problematical aspects of these ideas. At least: they were valued for white people; America's widespread domestic racism at this time – Jim Crow and so on – compromised her idealism here, more so than in Britain's case, where 'equality' was less central even to the rhetoric of her imperial enterprise. (We shall be returning to this.) In the case of the Philippines the argument for 'liberation' seemed the more convincing because the US was seizing the islands not from the natives, but from another empire: the Spanish. If this was imperialism, then it was of a special, *anti*-imperialist sort. Thereafter she 'liberated' the Filipinos by ruling them, in American ways.

Unfortunately some of the gloss was knocked off this when many native Filipinos turned out to be no more enamoured of America's new rule than they had been of Spain's, and fought a characteristically brutal war against it for fourteen years. (Modern Iraq obviously comes to mind.) This was one of the things that made America stop in her tracks, and held her back from much more formal imperialism after the Spanish war. (She carried on with the other kinds, however, right through the twentieth century: some very crude 'gunboat diplomacy', for example, especially in the western hemisphere.) It was a similar experience to Britain's after the Boer War. There is a famous remark of Theodore Roosevelt's, when he was offered the possibility of taking the Dominican Republic in 1904: that he had 'about the same desire to annex it as gorged boa-constrictor might have to swallow a porcupine wrong-end to'. The Spanish war had also provoked much anti-imperial sentiment in the country, especially in New England; interestingly, because (again) *old* England manifested the same phenomenon, and in a very similar form. It cannot be entirely coincidental that the 'theory of economic imperialism' was dreamt up by a Briton and an American, J. A. Hobson and Charles Conant, entirely independently of each other, so far as we can gather, and in precisely the same year: 1898. By some historians this anti-imperial tradition is supposed to express the true spirit of America, better than its brief imperialist fling. That may be so. ('Spirits' are notoriously difficult to pin down.) More likely, however, is that *both* features are equally characteristic of what was, in fact, a complex and ambivalent society and culture; exactly as they were in Britain's case.

Whether all that makes America an 'imperialist' power in the nineteenth century is debatable. It probably doesn't matter. ('Imperialism' *is* only a word, after all.) What does seem clear is that there are certain tendencies in American history, going right back to the nation's beginning, however significant they may or may not be compared with other trends, which can be *regarded* as imperialistic; have an imperialistic *potential* about them; and are very similar to features of certain other nations' histories at the same time, especially Britain's, which are generally *accepted* as imperialistic in these cases. The idea that America was entirely virginal in this regard is self-evidently ridiculous. She may still have been more chaste relative to others. Another possibility is that when she did 'sleep around' (I hope this doesn't sound sexist; the analogy would work as well, I think, if we could use the masculine pronoun for countries) she usually did it with better motives than other nations: out of pure love and affection, for example, or to do her partners some good. One may be right to be cynical of this. Personal gratification is a much likelier motive at least some of the time. 'Rape' seems a good term to use in many cases. (Here we definitely need the male word.) And it is possible to argue that some 'imperialist' characteristics were even *more* pronounced in her case than in others. But that does not matter to the general argument here. The point that needs to be made is not that the United States was particularly 'imperialistic' in the nineteenth century, but that she was not much *less* imperialistic than the countries she is often contrasted with. That is so, even if we take these protestations – about chastity, kind motives and the like – at face value. Britain in particular, as we saw, made almost precisely the same claims, both about her 'non-imperialism' during most of the nineteenth century, surprising as that might seem; and about the peculiar and unprecedented *benevolence* of her imperialism, by comparison with others', towards the end of the century, when that imperialism could no longer be denied. If you don't insist on getting in boats, and disregard God's word that he gave America to the Americans, it is easier to see the similarities between American 'expansion' and British 'imperialism' in the nineteenth century, than the differences.

Isolation

British imperialists saw them too. This was at the turn of the twentieth century, when Britain's imperial weakness drew some of them to the idea that America might be persuaded to share her imperial 'burden' with her, thus inspiring Kipling's famous poem, directed at President McKinley – the Spanish warrior. Later his successor, Theodore Roosevelt, showed great interest in the British Empire, and indeed many affinities with a certain kind of (radical) British imperialist. Cecil Rhodes, the great (and unscrupulous) millionaire empire-builder of the 1890s, often expressed the hope that Britain and the USA might someday be united again, this time with both in the imperial driving seat. That was why thirty-two of the Rhodes Scholarships to Oxford he endowed in his will were reserved for Americans.

After the First World War Lord Milner, Britain's ultra-imperialist British Colonial Secretary, still apparently thought that something like this was possible. The notion of making the defeated powers' (Germany's and Turkey's) colonial possessions into what were called 'mandated' territories, under the general supervision of the League of Nations, was largely the current US President Wilson's idea, and had been implemented at his insistence. Britain had no problem with that. As Colonial Under-secretary Leopold Amery told the House of Commons in 1920, none of the conditions set by the mandates differed in the slightest from those 'which we would impose upon ourselves, or which we have been in the habit of imposing upon ourselves whenever we dealt with subject peoples'. British imperial rule had *always* had the best interests of the latter at heart. For his part, Wilson did not appear to be an out-and-out anti-imperialist. For example, he had enthusiastically supported American annexation of the Philippines. (America still had the Philippines, of course.) The 'Fifth' of his famous 'Fourteen Points' of 1918 – the supposedly anti-imperialist one – in fact called for no more than an 'impartial adjustment' of colonial claims after the war that gave '*equal* weight' to the interests of colonial subjects with those of their colonial masters – no more. That seemed compatible with a liberal kind of imperialism. It was natural to infer from all this that America was prepared to shoulder at least some of the practical responsibility for administering *these* places (the mandates), at least. On this assumption, Milner was one of those who pressed for the Anglophile American G. L. Beer (rather than a Briton) to be Director of the new League of Nations Mandates Section. An Anglo-American imperium of some kind did not look entirely out of the question at this stage.

That dream was exploded, however, when the US withdrew from the League of Nations in 1920, leaving Britain and the other surviving colonial powers to shoulder the burden of administering the new territories on their own. How onerous that burden was, and the mess Britain for one made of it, has already been described. Some help from America could have been useful. One of the things it probably would have done was give Britain's colonial policy a moral nudge occasionally, to keep it more up to its idealistic mark. In her own major colony America certainly appears to have behaved quite idealistically, with major educational and legal reforms in the Philippines, a representative assembly from early on, and in 1935 full independence promised to the Filipinos within ten years. America's administration of the Philippines can be criticised on many grounds, not least for its economic exploitation of the islands, and its perpetuation of old ruling oligarchies; but it was generally libertarian according to America's (peculiar) lights. The same cannot be said for British colonial rule anywhere, unless libertarianism was forced on it. This is partly because America refused to get involved with the British Empire; though it would be mean, of course, to blame her for this, especially after her own experiences with it 150 years before. Instead she stood on the sidelines and carped. It was at this time that the 'anti-imperialist' part of her national history and ideology really kicked in. The First World War was mainly responsible for this, seen as it was – and not only in America – as the outcome of European competitive imperialisms. It had a very similar impact in Britain, as we saw, emphasising yet again the two countries' 'parallel' paths. But the manifestations of this impact were different. Because Britain already had an extensive empire, her revulsion was expressed through a kinder, more consensual kind of imperialism, or 'Commonwealthism' – in British *propaganda*, that is. In America it led to high-minded rejection: again, propagandistically. She became overtly 'anti-imperialist' for almost the first time.

This might have been helpful (to Britain), if America had carped at the right things. There was, as we have seen, a lot to be critical of in British interwar colonial policy: from the atrocity of Amritsar in 1919, to the general lethargy that informed most British 'development' policy in the more peaceful parts of the Empire for the next twenty years. Obviously there were individuals and organisations in America that took these themes up; though it has to be said that there was not much general American interest in European imperialism during this period, or, for that matter, in America's own colonial possessions – mirroring the situation in Britain at her earlier imperial peak. The growing imperialisms of Italy and Japan in the 1930s should also perhaps have been matters for greater concern than is easy to discern among the American people then; until, of course, it was too late to prevent the latter's deadly recoil on the American empire itself, at Pearl Harbor in Hawaii on 7 December 1941. But American isolation then really *meant* isolation. Disapproving of European imperialism she may have been; slightly hypocritically so, as we have argued, but nonetheless genuinely in the minds of most of her leaders. But she was not going to do anything to put European imperialism to rights. This was not the 'crusading' America of later years. Instead she concentrated on her own economic life and development. When her administrators did attack the British Empire, it was usually in connection with that.

What really got up the Americans' noses about the British Empire, it is clear from the statements and policies of the time, was its new post-1931 protectionism ('imperial preference').

Some officials got themselves into quite a lather about this. Cordell Hull, for example, Secretary of State from 1933 to 1944, called Britain's new imperial tariff structure 'the greatest injury, in a commercial sense, that has been inflicted on [America] since I have been in public life'. That – the harm done to American business interests – was obvious. What is interesting, however, especially to students of British imperialism, is that Hull also argued against it from general principle. Tariffs were the 'king of evils', and the root cause, he believed, of all wars. The President he served, Franklin D. Roosevelt, largely shared this view. Attentive readers of this book will recognise it immediately; it is pure Richard Cobden, and the basic idea, of course, that had lain behind British 'anti-imperialism' in the early and mid nineteenth century. For Britain the solution was 'free trade', for America the 'open door', which means roughly the same thing. That became a prime imperative of American foreign policy during the 1930s. British imperial preference was a direct challenge to that. This is what the US mainly meant by 'anti-imperialism'.

In both cases – Britain's in the nineteenth century, America's in the twentieth – this ideology clearly arose from their contemporary material circumstances. (This is quite irrespective of whether it may be 'right' or 'wrong'.) In Victorian Britain capitalists were one of the dominant interests in society, though not the only one. In twentieth-century America they were more dominant. Capitalism gives the clue as to why they both took this identical line over 'free trade' and the 'open door'; the different degrees of capitalist penetration in the two societies, on the other hand, explain some of the differences between them. For Britain, capitalism lay behind the extension of her empire, just as in America's case; but the way her empire was run thereafter owed more to other influential interests in her society, which the incompleteness of her capitalist revolution by comparison with America's had allowed to remain. This was partly why Britain ruled more overseas people directly and physically than America did – she had the class of men to do it (her upper-class paternalists); and also why she ruled them in ways that sometimes offended against the values associated with individualistic capitalism – because those values were alien to that class too. It also helps explain another difference: why the possibility of *free trade* capitalist imperialism occurred to some Britons before it occurred to Americans. If you are trapped within a free market discourse, convinced that the spread of trade is inevitably beneficent, and that the only true form of imperialism is that which restricts trade, then it is difficult to see the possible imperialist potential of a non-restrictive trade. Cobden and Hull clearly could not see it, for example; *had no conception* that free commerce – or capitalism, or 'business', or whatever – could have as controlling and oppressive an effect on other peoples as more conventional forms of empire. Britain's paternalists, with their snobbish distaste for capitalist enterprise of all kinds, always did have an inkling of this. Later socialists built on that. They did so in the US, too, with several attacks on American 'capitalist imperialism' being published there from the 1930s on. This kind of critique had a far shallower material base there, however, than in more hybrid Britain. Hence the idea that most Americans had at this time – very like British mid-Victorian liberals – that their country was intrinsically, systemically, anti-imperialist. Washing their hands of all new colonial responsibilities ('mandates') in 1920, and their general aloofness thereafter, probably helped confirm that.

Anti- (European) imperialism

That did not matter much to Britain while the US remained aloof. After December 1941, however, it mattered a lot. America was at last in the Second World War, drawn into it by that Japanese attack on her territory. That was a lifeline for Britain, who had originally declared war on Germany, of course, *without* being directly attacked. (Americans often regard their intervention in the Second World War as entirely altruistic; strictly speaking, however, Britain's was more so.) It always looked a hopeless task for her alone, against the far superior Nazi war machine. Her empire certainly wouldn't save her (though the dominions helped). So she needed the US. But the Americans were not at all happy about the British Empire. A famous article in *Life* magazine in October 1942 put bluntly what was then probably the predominant American view: 'one thing we are not fighting for is to hold the British Empire together.' President Roosevelt certainly agreed. 'He disliked British imperialism,' writes Roger Louis, 'pure and simple, as it seemed to him.' Many in his administration attributed the war itself to 'imperialism', and thought as a consequence that the ending of *all* imperialism should be one of the Allies' war aims. This naturally set up tensions between the USA and Britain; and between Roosevelt and Churchill – an arch-imperialist – in particular.

It looks like a dispute over fundamentals, but in fact it was not really as 'pure and simple' as this. Again, it is possible to see some convergence between the two sides' positions beneath the rhetorical surface. Britain felt that the Americans had it largely wrong about her empire, out of simple ignorance, compounded by what one commentator called 'the still persistent mentality of 1776'. This came out for example in Roosevelt's suggestion once that India model her interim government on the American 'Articles of Confederation' of 1781: 'the President's mind was back in the American War of Independence,' commented Churchill; and, more generally, in her insistence that 'independence' *à la* USA was the only acceptable form of 'liberation' for all colonial peoples, as against, say, full self-government within a larger unit like the Commonwealth, which might arguably have given some people more practical freedom than if they had to stand alone. There was also a great deal of irritation in Britain over the Americans' preaching tone: 'everything we produced on colonial subjects sounded like the Sermon on the Mount,' admitted one American critic; and their assumption that they were the only anti-imperialists in the world. (In fact, as Lord Hailey once pointed out to them, it was Britain that had invented the genre.) Of course this laid the Americans open to charges of self-righteousness and hypocrisy, which were largely deserved. People who live in glass houses shouldn't throw stones. Britons threw several back at them, including some that have been thrown already in this book: America's bloody colonisation of 'Indian' territory, for example; the war with Mexico; her imperial annexations of the 1890s; and – to bring the account right up to date – her treatment of her blacks. (Churchill once suggested that if the new United Nations was to be given the right to inspect British colonies, it might take a look at the American South too.) Still, this was something the British could work on. These were just misunderstandings. They could be put right. Hence the huge propaganda effort during the war years that was put into 'educating' the Americans as to the 'true' nature of the British Empire. To read much of that, you might wonder what the quarrel between them was really about.

It wasn't all bull. There were a number of common American misapprehensions about the Empire that could be easily and usefully corrected without departing at all from the truth, especially in the area of the Commonwealth. Some Americans, for example, didn't realise that the Australians were free. There was also the fact that there was a great deal of idealism, philanthropy, 'Sermon on the Mount' stuff in the history of the British dependent Empire too, certainly in its rhetoric, which was bound to appeal to the Americans once they learned about it. It wasn't all bad. Nor was it – as many of these propagandists gently reminded the Americans – all that different from their own historical experience, especially if the 'salt water fallacy' were scrapped. A quite convincing case could be made out of this for saying that the British Empire/Commonwealth was in fact a vehicle for *liberation*, not oppression. Jan Smuts, the Premier of

South Africa, even called it (in *Life* magazine, December 1942) 'the widest system of organised human freedom which has ever existed in human history', though that really must have seemed to be gilding the lily somewhat. A more convincing tactic was to frankly admit the flaws in the Empire, while insisting that these were aberrations and that Britain's intentions were good. That was the line adopted by many of these propagandists.

The problem with it, however, was that it didn't bear much scrutiny of the period of British colonial rule just before the war. It certainly didn't convince Roosevelt. Early in 1943 he undertook a tour of parts of Africa. The British colony he chose to visit was the Gambia, which was unfortunate, as it was probably the most neglected of all Britain's overseas possessions (though several others ran it close). It was 'a hell-hole', he told Churchill afterwards; 'it's the most horrible thing I have ever seen in my life. . . . The natives are five thousand years back of us. Disease is rampant. . . .' It would take a lot to persuade Roosevelt of Britain's good colonial intentions after that. (He never was persuaded.) The other factor countering all this rose-tinted propaganda, of course, was Churchill himself. He was clearly not one of the 'enlightened imperialists' portrayed in the propaganda. '"Hands off the British Empire" is our maxim, and it must not be weakened or smirched to please sob-stuff merchants at home or foreigners of any hue,' he thundered in December 1944; which was hardly designed to reassure American foreigners. No wonder the latter didn't trust the Brits. They were right not to.

The mistrust was mutual, and partly justified on the other side too. Many Britons – not only socialists, but also hardened old Foreign and Colonial Office hands – believed that behind America's anti-imperialist 'cant' lay a hidden agenda: to displace Britain as, in effect, the leading economic imperialist power in the world. It was this, they thought, that explained her hostility to 'Commonwealth' alternatives to complete colonial independence: even a free and voluntary Commonwealth might rival the

US commercially. It was the *size* of the British Empire that offended her. All that talk of 'liberation' and 'international trusteeship' for colonies was a 'cloak' or 'cover' for her own ambitions of *de facto* empire. Proof of this was the clear double standard she applied when it came to her own interests overseas, insisting both on extending them (especially in the Pacific) in the interests of 'security'; and on exempting them from the international supervision she demanded for every other country's overseas possessions. Her main rationales for this were, firstly, that America was so uniquely benevolent in her treatment of other peoples that she did not merit this kind of indignity; and secondly, that all these activities – especially her 'security' measures in the Pacific – were for the benefit not of herself alone, but of the 'world', especially world trade. This is yet another way in which, as Wm Roger Louis points out, America was copying nineteenth-century imperial Britain, though she doubtless didn't realise it. In Britain's case these kinds of argument are generally seen now as a mask for her self-aggrandisement, either consciously (which would make her hypocritical), or in a self-deluding kind of way. In the 1940s nearly everyone in the British government suspected the same of the US. This was largely justified. There were huge pressures within America for a postwar peace that would leave America strategically and commercially dominant. Indeed, few Americans denied it. Why should they, when American hegemony – the dominance of so intrinsically benevolent a power – was so clearly for the good of all the world?

Both countries' public stances on the question of empire, therefore, were tendentious, or at least faintly disingenuous; but in ways that could be seen to bring them together. There were real differences between them: over that 'independence versus self-government' thing, for example; the international scrutiny of colonies; and free trade versus imperial preference. Otherwise, however, America and Britain were either close, or else simply competitors or rivals for the same (imperial) prizes, rather than ideological enemies. So, the US accumulated its own vast network of military and naval bases in the world in much the same way as Britain had in the nineteenth century, and on the same conditions, ideally: that is, that they didn't involve the annexation of too much territory. ('These are not colonies,' said War Secretary Stimson; 'they are outposts.' Well . . .) Likewise, she did not object on principle to 'advanced' nations continuing to rule 'backward' ones, so long as it was on the clear understanding that it was with the ultimate self-rule of most of them in mind – apart that is from very primitive peoples, and those who happened to inhabit places felt to be of strategic value to America. She accepted that this would take some time; after all the Philippines, which she now held up as a model for other responsible colonial nations to follow, had needed more than forty years of tutelage to set them on the right path. Britain's public stance was very similar. She differed from the Americans over whether the Atlantic Charter, signed by Roosevelt and Churchill in August 1941, was intended to include the colonies in its general commitment to 'the right of all peoples to choose the form of government under which they will live' (Churchill claimed it only applied to countries liberated from Hitler). She also resisted US calls for her colonies to be subjected to international supervision, on much the same grounds as the Americans had refused it for theirs: namely, that she was too decent to require it. (Churchill also made the irrelevant point that as Britain was the only country that had entered the war for purely 'honourable' reasons, she did not deserve to be 'put into the dock' by 'a world we have tried to save'.) Both these positions became modified during the course of the war, however, with the Colonial Secretary giving a public pledge in July 1943 that 'self-government' was the ultimate aim for all the British colonies, albeit 'within the British Empire'. That narrowed the distance between the two powers.

Obviously that pledge had been forced on Britain – or on Churchill, at any rate; Clement Attlee, his Deputy, stood firmly in the Labour anti-imperial tradition, and was more genuinely in sympathy with the American line. But for whatever reason, America and Britain were converging fast. America was about to hugely extend her own empire of influence; Britain to let go – more quickly than anybody anticipated, as it happened, including the Americans – of her more formal one. Some saw this as the US stepping into Britain's old imperial shoes, albeit surreptitiously. The transfer was about to begin.

Flexing her muscles

First, however, there was a curious transitional stage, when America actually gave succour to the British Empire in many areas of the world, despite her earlier protestations, and in the face of her principles, as it would seem. This bears a slight resemblance to those old British imperial schemes for an Anglo-American 'white man's burden', though it was more one-sided (US-sided) than men like Kipling and Milner would probably have been happy with, and did not last for long. The main reason for it was the Soviet threat. America took some time to cotton on to that. Roosevelt seems never to have done so. Right up to his death he insisted that the major future danger to America and the world was a revival of old-fashioned western European imperialisms, especially British. If the analysis of this book is anywhere near correct – that is, of the British Empire's endemic weakness – he was quite seriously misled about that. Presidents Truman and Eisenhower, however, and the latter's Secretary of State John Foster Dulles, seem to have been wiser. The problem with the Soviets in this connection, however, was that they professed anti-imperialism too, and in an ideological form that was appearing more attractive to many discontented colonials than the American version. Unwilling to accept communism as a form of 'liberation', obviously because of the heavily capitalist bias of *their* notion of 'liberty', the Americans saw Soviet propaganda in the colonies mainly as an attempt to extend Russia's – or China's – own empires by stealth. That of course was the mirror image of the Soviets' perception of American foreign policy. A neutral way of looking at it would be to regard both of them as 'imperialisms' of a kind. Anyhow, this complicated the issue for the Americans. The choice now wasn't a simple one between European colonialism and freedom, but one between European colonialism, freedom, and communist colonialism. In this situation, people like Dulles felt they sometimes had to hold their noses, and go for the first.

It wasn't an unqualified backing, by any means. America picked and chose. Her long-term strategy was always to get rid of British imperialism: no doubt about that. Usually where she decided to shore up Britain's imperial defences it was in places of particular strategic importance to her, like Southeast Asia and the Middle East; or where she felt the natives weren't yet ready to embrace liberty (or her version of it); or where she didn't care much, as in tropical Africa, but hoped to get a quid pro quo from Britain in return. It was not always an easy call for her. Backing the British or any other empire might be the way to save colonial peoples from the clutches of communism; but there was also the danger that it could alienate them more. They were 'walking a tightrope', said Dulles in 1956, 'between backing Europe's empires and trying to win the friendship of countries escaping from colonialism'. This was a particular problem in the Arab world, vital of course to both countries for its oil, and where America's support for Israel (going back to Truman's recognition of the new state in 1948, against the advice of his Secretary of State) had already loaded the dice against her. It was their disagreement over this that led to the most spectacular breach between the two countries, in November 1956, when Eisenhower refused to support Britain's invasion of the Suez Canal Zone, and even threatened her with ruin (effectively) if she did not withdraw, because he calculated that it was better to have the Arabs on his side. It was around then, in fact, that the whole edifice of what Wm Roger Louis and Ronald Robinson call 'imperial Anglo-Americanism' began to crumble. Increasingly America called the shots on her own. The 'Anglo' arrangement had been just a stop-gap.

This freed America from the *trappings* of empire. Whether she stayed innocent of the essence of it is a moot point. Of course she wanted to believe so, for all the old reasons. 'Empire' was a dirty word in the American vocabulary. By it, however, Americans generally understood something very specific: a hankering for territory, one country ruling another. Leftists, of course, with their notion of 'economic' imperialism, were always sceptical of this narrow view. So should be historians of the British Empire, who have long been familiar with the similar idea of 'informal' empire, whether they are leftists or not. Informal empire means dominating countries by means short of outright rule or territorial control. As we saw in the last chapter, it was Britain's preferred way of going about her overseas business in the early and mid nineteenth century. What the Americans got up to in the last half of the twentieth century looks very much like this. Louis and Robinson, again, see it as returning imperialism 'to its original mid-Victorian design'. But you don't have to call it 'imperialism' if you don't want to. Americans clearly believed it was qualitatively different from the old, bad sort. Our old mid-Victorian friend Richard Cobden would almost certainly have agreed.

Really that doesn't matter. The aim of this book so far, to repeat, has been to show not so much that America was imperialistic, as that she was not much *less* imperialistic in her history than one other country, Britain, which is generally labelled imperialistic, even when she was not being much *more* imperialistic than America. (I hope that's clear.) In other words, they are comparable, whether as empires or not. American commercial and financial sway in the world in the second half of the twentieth century bears an obvious resemblance to Britain's in the nineteenth, whatever we want to label them. Both were widespread, enterprising, pushy, sometimes unscrupulous, and more successful than most other contemporary nations' investments and trades. Both were sometimes aided by their governments, though this was not supposed to be allowed in strict free trade theory. Each could lead to 'exploitation', in the pejorative sense of the word: that is, the abuse of human labour; especially where local people were needed to grow or extract the things Britain and America needed to import, or – latterly – to manufacture goods cheaply for them, like Nike shoes. British and American economic enterprise were followed, inevitably, by British and American fashions and cultures: shirts, ties and even tweeds in nineteenth-century India, jeans and trainers all over the world a hundred years later; plus the 'cuppa', Coke, jazz, the novel, Hollywood films, cricket and football, Christianity, swearing, and so on. In neither case, incidentally, was there as much acculturation in the other direction as one might expect: 'Eastern' ideas and institutions catching on in Britain and America; though there were some exceptions, especially (late on) in the area of food. This is clearly a sign of cultural dominance, if not necessarily of cultural imperialism. It suggests a certain arrogance on the part of the dominating nation, which might be labelled 'imperial'; but it could also indicate a degree of *receptivity* from the 'Eastern' side of the equation which, in my view at least, detracts from this. The same can be said for a great deal – probably the majority – of Britain's nineteenth-century and America's twentieth-century overseas trade: the sort, that is, that relied on the simple sale and purchase of goods. That *was* 'free'. People bought British and American products because they wanted – even craved – them. Even by its least 'formal' definition, 'imperialism' surely requires some degree of force or pressure to be exerted. 'Pressure' of course is a slippery concept. There can be arguments over some of the subtle forms of it that certain purely commercial practices (especially monopolisation, but also advertising) involve. Generally, however, these pressures were too weak to justify the term 'imperialist' in most of these cases (by my definition). We need more than that; for example, an Opium War.

The US has never had an Opium War, exactly. (No one suggests that the massive increase in opium cultivation that followed her invasion of Afghanistan in 2001 was one of the motives for that attack.) The nearest she got to this was probably when her tobacco industry in 1990 succeeded in forcing the Thai government to lift a ban on the import of American cigarettes that it had imposed for health reasons: not with gunboats, this time, but through threats from the World Trade Organization (WTO). That is qualitatively similar: for example, in putting freedom of trade before local wishes, and also, perhaps, in the lethalness of the product involved.

The means by which it was done, however, signals a significant divergence between British trade policy in the nineteenth century and American in the twentieth. Britain had a similar 'free trade' agenda; but she didn't try to enforce it worldwide. She embraced free trade herself and in her dependencies, unilaterally. She negotiated bilateral treaties with other independent nations to establish it between her and them. (Technically, this was what the Opium Wars were fought over; not 'free trade' *per se*, but China's breach of a free trade *treaty* with Britain.) She hoped that other nations would follow her moral example when they saw the benefits it was bringing to Britain: as for a time many of them did. But she did not cajole and threaten, as twentieth-century America did; *retaliate* when other nations declined to 'open' their 'doors' to her, for example; or try to enforce the system on the world through her domination of agencies like the WTO, International Monetary Fund (IMF) and World Bank. (Nor, it might be said, was nineteenth-century Britain quite as hypocritical as America – and also Europe – became later, in preaching free trade for others while protecting the very domestic industries, usually agriculture, that poorer countries might benefit from being allowed to compete freely with.) In other ways, too, Britain never had modern America's economic clout: though partly, it has been argued, because the latter is more willing to tolerate huge deficits than was Britain. (Emmanuel Todd, for one, thinks that makes her vulnerable.) Britain also never had a military as huge as America's; or a secret army (in effect) as potent and ruthless (Chile, Guatemala . . .) as the CIA. For all these reasons, the comparison that is sometimes made between British nineteenth-century and American twentieth-century 'imperialisms', and the idea that the latter simply stepped into the same-sized shoes of the former, are misleading. In terms of sheer global muscle the US was far more dominant, and therefore in some senses more 'imperial', than her predecessor ever was. Patrick O'Brien characterises the difference as one between 'primacy' (the British position) and 'hegemony'. America is the first modern hegemon, imperial or otherwise.

Many Americans also believed there was another difference. We have seen this anticipated before: for example, when the US took all those islands in the Pacific. They did that, they insisted, not in their own selfish interests alone, but for the good of the whole world. It was the same with hegemony. Unlike past empires, America was seeking the benefit of all. She thought she was unique in history in this, though she certainly was not; or at least, not in this *perception* of herself. It is possible to think of several other empires in history, including the British, and even the Soviet, whose aficionados also thought they were uniquely wonderful in this way. That doesn't, of course, mean that they couldn't have been wrong, and America right. Later on her sense of rightness was greatly boosted when the Soviet Union, her main ideological as well as military rival, collapsed in 1989 (the fall of the Berlin Wall), which was widely taken to prove the superiority of her 'free' model over all others. One influential scholar – influential probably because he told people what they wanted to hear – announced that the 'End of History' had arrived then, no less: that is, history's culmination, the moment (literally) of truth, when all false political religions fell away. This confidence in their system, and in the inevitability of its eventual triumph, is another thing that twentieth-century Americans shared with many nineteenth-century Britons, but then – as with 'hegemony' – took to much greater lengths. You find it in many of the mid-Victorian English middle classes, but also *challenged* then by the survival of upper-class paternalistic values, and by working- (or intellectual middle-) class socialism; and beginning to fade as the nineteenth century drew to its end. More Americans, on the other hand, appear to have been morally certain that they had got it right, not only for themselves, but for humankind generally.

There are two problems with this. The first, of course, is that they might *not* have got it right (or that there isn't such a thing as 'right' in this connection). In that case her hegemony is bound to appear less benevolent. We shall return to this in the next chapter; it is a contentious issue, naturally. Less contentious is the second problem: that it is sometimes difficult to square the conduct of her foreign policy in these 'Cold War' years with even her own conception of 'rightness'. First of all there was her support for the hated British Empire (and for others), which we have mentioned already. Even when she dropped that, however, all was not democratic sweetness and light. It is universally accepted today – it was often denied at the time – that she bolstered some dreadful foreign dictators in defence of her interests; plotted covertly to remove democratically elected leaders whom she thought might not be sufficiently pro-American; even backed 'terrorism' if it suited her agenda; and got involved in several dozen wars all over the world, some of them unsavoury, two of them large-scale (Korea and Vietnam), and one of them (the latter) a disaster in its outcome for her. One of the results of all this was millions of dead. These do not seem to be the actions of a standard-bearer for 'freedom'. The support for dictators, in particular, is another thing marking her off from Britain in the nineteenth century; this was not generally a tactic of the latter, though possibly only because, as a formal imperial power, she was able to provide her own dictators – hopefully more benevolent ones. America didn't have this luxury.

This American way *could* be squared with 'freedom'; but only by seeing 'communism' as the main threat to it, which from Truman to Reagan was the consistent American line. The existence of a hugely armed Soviet Union as a powerful counterbalance to America, and then of the People's Republic of China, exacerbated this, and was what was supposed to legitimise America's enormous military (and nuclear) build-up in these years; the CIA plotting; and all those overseas military bases – 702 (*seven hundred and two*) in 130 countries by one recent count. (The 'supposed' is there because of the suggestion that President Eisenhower once famously voiced, that much of it could be special pleading by the 'military-industrial complex'.) The Sino-Soviet threat was thought to justify almost any means to prevent this kind of 'democracy' (both sides appropriated the word, of course) spreading. Just as the British Empire had once been, a Saudi prince or Iranian Shah was preferable to communism, even if 'liberty' might have been the best alternative of all. And, naturally, we must not forget the US's oil interests. That was why communism was feared in the Middle East, in particular. Oil, of course – a material interest – is what *defines* US foreign policy as 'imperialistic' for those who believe the crucial factor behind imperialism is mercenary gain.

Comparisons and contrasts

The idea that America's history has been significantly less 'imperialistic' than Britain's, therefore, is clearly a myth. This isn't an original point; I imagine that most serious historians today, on both sides of the Atlantic, acknowledge America's 'imperialist' past, though they might not realise how precisely similar to Britain's many aspects of it were. In the earlier nineteenth century one can see British and American 'colonisation' following the same path almost exactly, so long as one puts out of one's mind the 'salt water' thing. Mid-nineteenth century attitudes to 'imperialism' were surprisingly similar. Both countries experienced assertively imperialistic 'aberrations' at the end of the nineteenth century; the main difference here is that it came to be *regarded* as an aberration in America's case, whereas in Britain's it has been taken to be typical. After the First World War the differences between them were mainly rhetorical. Britain acknowledged her empire (as of course she was bound to), America took up the banner of anti-imperialism; but for America this was all words – she did nothing practical to try to end imperialism; and on most practical colonial issues, including the conditions, timing and so on of self-government for subject peoples, their leaders thought along exactly the same lines. After the Second World War the two powers found themselves in imperial harness for a while. It really is difficult to argue for an absolutely innocent non-imperial America on the basis of all this.

There *were* differences; but they might be thought to be secondary, or even in some cases to strengthen America's 'imperial' credentials. It is true that for most of the past 200 years the USA has been genuinely dead against annexing and ruling countries, though this also allies her, as we have seen, with people who in Britain's case are regarded as 'informal' imperialists, at least. We should expect this; it is a clear characteristic of the liberal capitalism which the Americans tended to go for more enthusiastically, and stay with longer, than Britons. It is also an outcome of America's different social system, which had much less room in it for the 'ruling class' and its ethos that Britain relied on so much to actually run her colonies, and also incidentally to protect them, in so far as they could, from liberal capitalist predators. There is of course a good principled reason for it, too: that it is simply *wrong* for one nation to rule another (the narrow definition of 'empire'). On the other hand it could be said to have a down side. If you want to force your will on other countries – for whatever reason, bad or good – it doesn't leave many options open to you. War is one; but that is a somewhat crude instrument, and damaging in some very obvious ways (all those people killed). In America's case, it may also have encouraged a masculinist, 'macho' ethic, further boosted by all that popular imperialist literature ('Westerns'), which differed at least marginally from Britain's more 'paternalist' imperial ethos. Soldiers are only required to bash people; fathers ('pater') are supposed to understand and look after them. Surrogates are another less than satisfactory alternative to 'rule'. If you have a foreign interest you feel you need to secure, don't trust local democracies to do it for you, and if you have repudiated annexation, then the only thing left to you may be bolstering local tyrants, who might not have the same scruples as you. You can't control a Shah like you can a Viceroy. That may be problematical.

This is why America's informal methods of exerting control were not necessarily less tyrannical than a more formal imperialism might have been. (This, however, should not be taken as an argument for the latter. There are alternatives. We shall return to this towards the end of this book.) We have touched on other differences between her imperialism and Britain's in this chapter also: America's greater 'hegemony', for example; her very special understanding of the notion of 'freedom'; her sense of national uniqueness and destiny ('exceptionalism'); and so on. All this *coloured* her imperialism (or whatever) in a different way from Britain's. Whether it made her more or less 'imperialistic' is debatable. It's not really important. There was certainly plenty of 'imperialist' *potential* here.

3

'We don't do empire'
American 'imperialism' after 9/11

No desire to dominate

The big argument over American 'imperialism' broke out after '9/11', the Al-Qaeda attacks on New York and Washington in 2001; to which the US responded by invading two foreign countries, Afghanistan in October 2001 and Iraq in March 2003. On the surface this bore many resemblances to the imperialism of the nineteenth century, especially the British, which is one reason why the charge was made. America's leaders rejected it, of course, as they were bound to in view of their national mythology. We have quoted Rumsfeld on this already, in the Introduction (and in the title of this chapter). He was echoed by Vice-President Dick Cheney: 'if we were a true empire we would currently preside over a much greater piece of the earth's surface than we do. That's not the way we operate'; and by the President himself, George W. Bush, in his 2004 State of the Union Address: 'we have no desire to dominate, no ambitions of empire.' That was unequivocal. Slightly less so might be thought to be the subtle distinction that Condoleezza Rice, Bush's National Security Advisor (later Secretary of State), made between 'imperial', which she accepted the US was, perforce, and imperial*ist*, which she thought was something else entirely. This looks casuistical, but in fact is a valid theoretical distinction. 'Imperial' describes a state, a situation; 'imperialist' a policy. It was the idea that the US was out to extend her power for her own ends, as a matter of policy, that these people wanted to quash. That, of course, is what they pictured all previous empires in history doing, including the British; in that case wrongly.

Away from the politicians, the 'e' and 'i' words featured more positively in analyses of these events, by journalists, for example, and academics. Hostile commentators used them to warn America of what she might be getting herself into: exactly what she had thought she had spent her whole history trying to avoid. Supportive ones generally argued that, yes, this was 'empire', possibly even imperial*ism*; but that it was an entirely different sort of empire from what had gone before. Generally they regarded it as more benevolent. 'America is the most magnanimous of all imperial powers that have ever existed,' wrote Dinesh D'Souza, in an article entitled 'In praise of American empire' (2002). William E. Odom and Robert Dujarric thought she 'differ[ed] fundamentally from all past empires' in not being 'dominating'. That was in a book called *America's Inadvertent Empire* (2004). Unfortunately most of these claims were made on the basis of almost no knowledge of any 'past empires' at all, including Britain's. (Odom and Dujarric's long bibliography, for example, includes not a single work on any of the American empire's predecessors.) That seems an odd way of going about showing that something is new.

The argument of this chapter will be that the modern American empire, if you want to call it that, *is* different from at any rate the British Empire; but not in some of the ways it is usually taken to be. In a nutshell: many of America's present-day underlying motives are comparable to Britain's in the nineteenth century, as are the way their empires have come about ('inadvertently'). They are similar in what *I* regard as their 'dominance'; and also – strikingly – in their contemporary *denials* of that dominance ('we don't do empire': cf. Gladstone). They may possibly differ in the balance between them of 'idealistic' and 'mercenary' motives, though I am not sure to which nation's credit. (It partly depends on how 'idealistic' you think certain 'ideals' are.) In most ways, therefore, it is more convincing to see the present-day American 'empire' as standing in a direct line with the British than as something new and unique. The major differences between them are, firstly, the extent of America's 'hegemony', which we have mentioned already; secondly, the territorial thing – her greater reluctance to directly annex countries; thirdly, the amazingly ambitious 'vision' she embraced for her imperialism in the early twenty-first century; and lastly, 9/11. These are genuine differences, albeit rather less straightforward – more complex and ambivalent – than they may seem. There are also significant divergences in the ways the two countries have implemented their imperial designs, deriving partly from changing international circumstances, but also from the disparate elements in their domestic cultures. Not all these distinctions, I think, necessarily favour America, in the sense of making her less 'imperialistic' than previous imperial powers, or more imperially beneficent.

The new American century

The event that really established America's hegemony took place a few years before 9/11. That was the fall of the Berlin Wall in 1989; or rather, the collapse of the Soviet empire that it symbolised. This had two broad effects. The first was to lift a restraint on America's power. As everyone at the time said: she was now the world's sole superpower. She was also the world's *first* sole superpower. Britain was certainly not a precedent here. Even at her imperial zenith (whenever that was), the latter had been nothing like so dominant, except possibly in the area she chose to concentrate on (outside Europe). She had always had powerful rivals. Even the Roman Empire had only been hegemonic in the 'known' world of the time (known to Europe, that is). So this was absolutely new. It looked as though America could do anything she wanted in the world. On the other side, the emasculation of the Russian Bear also meant, or seemed to, that she no longer had to do some of the nasty things that she had felt were needed before then to combat communism, like shoring up unpleasant dictators, and plotting against dodgy democrats. She could use her great power and influence more benevolently. Alternatively, if she wanted to, she could retreat into comfortable isolation again. It should have been the dawn of a bright new age for her.

Isolationism looked a possibility for a time. George W. Bush was clearly uninterested in foreign affairs – even foreign countries – when he became President in 2001, and notoriously ignorant of them. (This was revealed when he was ambushed in a CBS television interview in February 2000 with a series of quite simple questions on the names of world leaders, and flunked them all.) He was also publicly critical of his predecessor Clinton's 'humanitarian' foreign interventions; as was his close adviser Condoleezza Rice, who let it be known that *she* thought America's foreign policy in the future should be limited to the defence of her 'national interest', narrowly defined. That included pushing for trade liberalisation, but little more. It sounded like a return to the 1920s. This put the wind up Britain's Tony Blair – an 'imperialist' before Bush ever was – as we shall see. On the other hand, there was a contrary trend in contemporary Republican thinking, called 'neo-conservative'; represented by an organisation called the 'Project for the New American Century', whose agenda (set as early as 1997) was 'a foreign policy that boldly and purposefully promotes American principles abroad' – not just 'interests'; 'and national leadership that accepts the United States' global responsibilities'. It also argued for 'full spectrum dominance' by America, which was defined as being able 'to defeat any adversary and control any situation across the range of military operations' – quite an ambition. On the face of it that seemed to have rather more 'imperialist' potential. Whether it would have come to anything but for 9/11 is impossible to say.

This is one of the problems with assessing the degree of America's 'imperialism' after then: that she had 9/11 to hide it behind. That was of course a monstrous attack on her, though possibly not as dangerous as it was presented; which clearly called for defensive measures, and might even justify retributive ones. Self-defence is usually considered to be *not* the same as imperialism. The first of America's post-9/11 wars, the invasion of Afghanistan, could plausibly be justified as a defensive action, on the grounds that the Afghan government of the time had harboured and was still harbouring the perpetrators of the atrocity. That, however, doesn't mean that the Americans might not have had an imperialist agenda in Afghanistan *as well*. The second invasion, of Iraq, seemed less justifiable on grounds of self-defence, simply because Saddam Hussein, the Iraqi dictator, almost certainly had *not* aided Al-Qaeda, and, as it turned out, posed no military threat to the US in any other way. On the other hand, the US might have *thought* otherwise; which could be considered to acquit it of imperialist motives over this too.

There can be no doubt – it is proved by opinion polls – that the majority of the American *people* believed that by going to war against Saddam Hussain they were hitting back at the perpetrators of 9/11. That was foolish; but for this the distortions and pusillanimity of their news media were largely to blame. The only queries must be over the thinking of the administration at the time. Was it really as convinced as it said it was by the intelligence it claimed it had of Saddam's links with Osama bin Laden and Iraq's stockpile of weapons of mass destruction ('WMDs')? Or was this just an attempt to jump-start the plans for 'regime change' in the Middle East that had lain on the drawing board of the Project for the New American Century for some years now? It may be too early yet to answer this question with any certainty.

In any case it may not be an easy one to answer even when all the facts become known. 'Administrations' are made up of different interests and sets of motivations, and of individual people whose own motives may be mixed and confused. We can see this in the case of many nineteenth-century British imperial wars; it is why there is still so much controversy over their 'causes'. Partly, it depends on who you think is 'manipulating' whom. The problem with an entirely cynical reading of these later (American) events is that it may underestimate the gullibility of certain people; and what *looks* to be the basic honesty of, for example, Secretary of State Colin Powell, who seemed 'genuine' when he presented his 'evidence' for Iraqi WMDs before the General Assembly of the United Nations in February 2003. (Apart from anything else, would he have deliberately risked the embarrassment that both he and America were bound to suffer when the flaws in that 'evidence' were revealed?) Also, we may not need to draw a rigid distinction between foolishness and Machiavellian deception here; politicians are perfectly capable of fooling *themselves* into believing what others are telling them, or what they want to think. That is obviously true of the weaker, stupider ones. If there was any deliberate duplicity in this case, it probably did not come from the President.

The 9/11 attack is clearly a special factor here, not found to anything like the same degree in Britain's case. As it happens, Britain also experienced 'terrorism' at her late nineteenth-century imperial zenith – firstly Irish (or, more correctly, American-Irish), and secondly 'Anarchist' – albeit of a milder, because less efficient, kind. This may have been an element in the general atmosphere of apprehension that lay behind the 'new' British imperialism of those years, but there were no direct links between them – between Fenians and Boers, for example; even fewer than between Saddam and Osama bin Laden. In any case the British government's response here was very different: not to bomb the places that were harbouring the terrorists (it would have had to be Boston, Mass.), but, in effect, to try to 'appease' the latter, by offering Irish 'home rule'. Going further back, there may be a precedent for the *shock* of 9/11 in the outbreak of the Indian 'Mutiny' in 1857; but this is stretching things a bit. (Here the British response was initially vengeful, but ultimately more lenient.) In all essential respects, the Al-Qaeda attacks were a unique feature of this modern manifestation of 'imperialism' (or whatever). It is possible that without them, the latter would not have happened at all.

It can also be argued however – conversely – that 9/11 could not have happened without American imperialism; that essentially what the attacks on the Twin Towers represented was a form of 'blowback' – Chalmers Johnson's word – against America for all the 'informal' and covert imperialism she had inflicted on the world before then, much of it regarded as 'bullying' in character, especially (so far as Al-Qaeda was concerned) in the Middle East. The credibility of this idea may be thought to be strengthened by the fact that Johnson had actually predicted something like this – though not, of course, the precise form the 'blowback' took – long before 9/11, and for this reason. As has happened before in history – Gladstone's invasion of Egypt, to put down a local revolt against other forms of Western dominance there, is a good example – one kind of imperialism was provoked by a reaction to another kind. Few Americans were able to see this, and indeed felt understandably hurt when the point was put to them at the time. There was a famous onslaught on the *London Review of Books* in October 2001, for example – American subscriptions cancelled, one letter-writer threatening to 'shove your lefty loony faces into some dog shit' on his next visit to London (he later apologised) – after one contributor suggested that *some people might feel* about 9/11 that 'the United States had it coming' to her (not that it was true). This, however, was more a reflection of the American people's ignorance of how their country was behaving abroad, and of how it was perceived, than anything else. (Again, their media were much to blame.) Many people outside the US, and doubtless some Americans (certainly Chalmers Johnson), hoped it would lead to a degree of self-reflection along these lines, once the shock and pain of the atrocity had subsided. The Bush administration, as is by now well known, did not take this option, preferring instead to attribute the attacks to 'hatred' of American 'freedoms', and simple 'evil'. That, of course, was less likely to divert America from her 'imperialist' path.

In any case, even when every allowance is made for American shock, poor intelligence, the desire for blind revenge, and simple misjudgement, it is difficult to see the Iraq War as *just* a response to 9/11. In fact few people pretended it was. At least three other motives clearly came into it, for all of which British imperial antecedents can be found. The first was the 'unfinished business' factor: George Bush Junior was finishing off what his father had started when *he* had invaded Iraq in 1991, to free Kuwait from Saddam's aggression. On that occasion Bush Senior had not gone on to remove Saddam from power, leaving the latter crowing. Junior completed the job (though there's no evidence that Daddy wanted him to). That seems petty, but it may have had some influence. The best British imperial precedent for it is probably the invasion of the Sudan in 1898 to make up for Gladstone's pusillanimity in surrendering it (and sacrificing the national hero General Gordon) to the 'Mahdi' in 1885. A second widely suspected motive – a bigger one – was oil. Iraq had masses of that, of course, and gas-guzzling America was thought to need it. That was a *very* imperialist factor, if it really was crucial. Bush and Cheney's own American oil industry backgrounds and connections fuelled this suspicion, inevitably; especially when Cheney's old company – Halliburton – was awarded some of the juiciest contracts in post-invasion Iraq. For British precedents for that we do not need to go beyond mid twentieth-century Iraq itself. The third general motive was the 'liberal' one. This was the main one bruited by the administration, especially when those WMDs didn't turn up. Iraq had been invaded (a) to free it from a murderous tyrant, and (b) to establish democracy in the region. Aficionados of the 'oil conspiracy' theory didn't generally go along with that, but there is no reason to doubt the genuineness of this motive in the minds of many of those in positions of influence in Washington in 2003. Nor is it necessarily incompatible with the 'oil' one. In the old British Empire 'commerce' and 'civilisation' often travelled in harness, as we have seen. Oil and democracy could be similarly linked. For America before 2001 they generally hadn't been, even rhetorically (*vide* the US's support of Saudi Arabia's sheikhs, to secure her oil for her). But the case could be made.

Beyond and behind this, however, there was something more: a new, broader vision of America's general foreign policy objectives, which the attacks of 9/11 had triggered, or enabled. No one denied this, or tried to keep it secret; it was out there in the open – on the Project for the New American Century's website, for example – for all to see. Indeed, this was supposed to be one of the distinguishing features of the new (Bush Junior) administration's foreign policy, by contrast with what were presented by the Republicans as Clinton's aimless, shortsighted and 'humanitarian' – a word they much derided – thrashing about. The Republicans by contrast would be focused, clear-sighted, consistent, decisive and strong. To a certain right-wing mentality, of course, these characteristics are virtues in themselves. (They are supposed to constitute what is known as 'leadership'.) More important, however, was the specific content of this philosophy; which, it should be emphasised at the start, was not an ignoble one. Those who took it to be a mere cloak for 'lower' or more mercenary motives were probably preventing themselves from understanding it fully. This does not necessarily make it any the less imperialistic, however, by any but the most hostile or pedantic definitions of the word. It envisioned America remoulding the world. That would count as 'imperialism' in most people's books.

The city on a hill

It was an extraordinary ambition; but it should not have been entirely unexpected. The idea of America as an *example* to the rest of the world – or even *the* example – goes back a very long way. John Winthrop famously saw the Puritan settlements of New England as 'a Citty upon a Hill', with 'the eies of all people . . . uppon us' in 1630. That, incidentally, was originally intended as a warning to those same settlers not to stray from God's laws, lest 'wee shall open the mouthes of enemies to speak evill of the wayes of god'. The same notion can be found running through her history thereafter, albeit unevenly; expressed, for example, in Thomas Jefferson's belief that eventually the American system would spread everywhere – 'to some parts sooner, to others later, but finally to all' – because it was the expression of universal rationality. Benjamin Franklin called America's cause 'the cause of all mankind'. Woodrow Wilson was another who believed that 'American principles, American policies' were 'also the principles and policies of forward-looking men and women everywhere, of every modern nation, of every enlightened community. They are the principles of mankind and must prevail.' And so on. Sometimes, in reading such statements, one gets the impression that Americans believed – and perhaps still do – that they had *invented* democracy, quite alone, and were solely responsible for its spread in the world, either though example or by intervention (like, later, in 1941). Then, coming into the later twentieth century, the 'City upon a Hill' phrase was revived again, this time much more arrogantly than in Winthrop's cautionary version, and often with a 'Shining' in front of it, to describe this essential place of America's in the world. In the 1940 war film *The Fighting 69th*, for example, starring James Cagney, it appears in the final patriotic epilogue. Ronald Reagan was unconscionably fond of the phrase; he probably got it – like much of the rest of his American mythology – from the movies. It was also Reagan who once described America as 'the last best hope of man on earth'. Such rhetoric was not confined to Republicans; it was, after all, Madeleine Albright, President Clinton's Secretary of State, who characterised America as 'the indispensable nation. We stand tall, and we see further into the future.' But it seemed to come more easily to Republicans, and especially the 'Neocons'. Condoleezza Rice, for example, described the United States as 'on the right side of history' and claimed that 'American values are universal'. 'History' was often invoked here, especially after the collapse of one alternative reading of it – the Marxist dialectic – in the 1980s. It was a favourite line of Clinton's, too. Then, in the early twenty-first century, religion made a comeback, with America being seen as *God's* chosen nation, no less, very like Israel in olden times. George W. Bush combined the two lines in 2000 when he claimed, remarkably, that the USA had been 'chosen by God and commissioned by history to be a model to the world'. That is one hell of a claim to make for any nation. But so far it is not a threatening one. A 'model' is just that: a template, or a plan to follow. Shining cities should attract by their own light. You would expect that to happen, naturally, if the light really was so bright and seductive.

This bears similarities with nineteenth-century liberal thought in Britain, though with rather more 'God' than was common there, unless this was just because the Victorian British wore their religion less on their sleeves – it is arguable that the latter were better *Christians* underneath, at least of the Gospels (gentle Jesus) kind – and also, probably, more national self-confidence. Britons also liked to believe that they were in the van of what they called 'progress', but they were not so sure that they had achieved perfection yet, or even knew for certain what it was. The analogy they preferred, rather than the 'City', was a 'path'; Britain was further along the 'freedom' road that every people would follow eventually, but certainly not at its end. This probably had much to do with their national mythology, which saw British freedom as a *process*, being steadily worked out historically (the 'Whig' view, it is often called), rather than as something established all (or nearly all) at one go, at a single moment (1776/87) in the past. In both cases, however, the clear implication was that there was no need to force this on other people. They would follow, initially as individuals (both countries attracted immigrants) and then as entire nations, when they saw how free, prosperous and happy Britons were along their road, or Americans in their 'Citty'. All that was needed was the example; human rationality would do the rest.

There was another similarity. Both creeds put great weight on 'free trade': not only as a good in itself, producing and diffusing material prosperity, for example; but also as a trigger for the achievement of other kinds of public good. Richard Cobden had believed that other 'freedoms' would follow the spread of free trade, almost inevitably; that this simple idea was the key to the salvation of the world in almost every way. So did the later American 'Neocons'. Most of these invariably bracketed 'markets and democracy' together when they spoke and wrote of their hopes for the future; in many cases these two words were placed in this order, with 'markets' coming first, because that was seen as crucially enabling the second, rather than vice versa. Condoleezza Rice, in an influential *Foreign Affairs* article of early 2000 (before Bush II's election, therefore), wrote of her 'faith in the power of markets and economic freedom to drive political change'; a faith, she claimed, that was 'confirmed by experiences around the globe'. This reads like pure Cobden. It was clearly the ideological justification – there will have been more practical and perhaps less savoury reasons also – for the haste with which the US, whenever she conquered countries in this post-9/11 period, set about instituting free markets, privatisation and so on there, usually to the benefit of American companies, long before establishing 'democracies', which might have taken another line over these questions. This appeared curious – even anti-democratic – to other kinds of democrats. Surely people should be allowed to choose their own economic arrangements, as well as everything else? But it was not, of course, if you assumed that markets and other sorts of freedom were inextricably linked; as in a capitalist-dominated democracy you were likely to.

For nineteenth-century British liberals this was not so much of a problem, because 'democracy' was less of a priority, even propagandistically. This was not unreasonable, by their lights. There is no *necessary* connection between democracy and other kinds of political liberalism, at least in logic; you can have democratically elected tyrannies, for example, and non-elective autocracies that are nonetheless more sensitive to most human freedoms than those. In the mid-nineteenth century they also feared democracies being hijacked by uneducated rabbles, as during the French revolutionary Terror; or – and this was the objection some of them had to the American system – by rich and powerful interest groups. For Cobden and his ilk the freedoms that were supposed to come in the wake of trade liberalisation were subtly different, or given a different emphasis: freedom from want for everyone, which implied a degree of egalitarianism; freedom from being killed in war – there were strong elements of pacifism and anti-militarism in mid-Victorian liberal thought; and freedom from the state, which was often taken to mean the end *of* states as such, or true 'internationalism' – for Cobdenism tended to be antipathetic to nationalism and even patriotism, too. This was 'liberal' imperialism as it was understood during the mid-nineteenth century; by those, that is, who accepted that it was 'imperialism' at all.

Just to list these characteristics is to point up some of the differences between then and later; for American neo-conservative free marketeers were not egalitarian or pacifist or anti-patriotic in the least. In fact it had been a very long time since economic liberals generally were. One of the most interesting developments in the history of Anglo-American political thought during the course of the twentieth century was the one that led to the separation of the two *kinds* of 'liberal' over this period: so that concepts of freedom that had used to be associated together now found themselves on opposite sides of the political debate. In Britain this culminated in Margaret Thatcher's philosophy of a 'free economy in a strong state', which would have been incomprehensible to her mid-Victorian predecessors. In modern America it is exemplified in the obloquy that attaches to the very word 'liberal' in right-wing free-market circles. Like Thatcher, the Neocons were keen on 'strength': a punitive penal code, for example; a large military; and a powerful sense of state- or nationhood, generally referred to as 'patriotism'. They also had little compunction about trying to spread 'free trade' (or the 'open door', or 'globalisation') *forcibly*; which was the major difference between them and the Cobdenites, in theory at least. The latter had fondly believed that force would prove unnecessary – enlightenment would spread 'naturally'; but, as Andrew Bacevich writes, 'only the most devout disciple of Adam Smith would count on the market's "invisible hand" to keep order' now. It was this collection of 'hard' libertarian values that had the potential, at least, to transform what would otherwise have been a merely liberal foreign policy ideology into an aggressive liberal-*imperialist* one. The closest historical comparisons – combining patriotism, militarism and 'enlightenment' – are probably Napoleon's imperialism, and the expansionary Soviet Union. The nineteenth-century British imperial parallel is less close.

Still, it was not inevitable that all that 'City on a Hill' stuff, even in this tougher guise (in some versions it appears as the *Citadel* on the Hill), should turn imperialistic. Before 9/11 it looked as though the 'shining' was working well enough on its own. The attractions of certain manifestations of American capitalism and culture worldwide were famous (or notorious): from the nostrums of the Harvard Business School, through to Coca-Cola, Levi's jeans and McDonald's. A term coined for this was 'soft power'. America looked to be seducing the globe with its products, and 'liberating' it at the same time. She had faced down Soviet communism: the last serious challenge to her ideology and hegemony. The world was moving in a capitalist direction, quite massively, especially in the old Soviet territories, albeit with some stragglers. All Americans had to do was sit back and wait for the process to work itself out. Very few of them, even Republicans – *especially* Republicans, perhaps, for they tended to be more literally 'conservative' than Democrats – believed that it was America's role to spread 'freedom' in any more active and forcible ways. That after all was not – supposedly – how the Cold War had been won. It should have been unnecessary.

What suddenly made it seem necessary was a combination of 9/11 and the new administration – and new *sorts* of Republicans – that came to power in America in 2001. The events of 9/11 had the effect of pushing America's lines of defence outwards. The 'homeland' could no longer be shielded from terrible dangers merely parochially and passively – even with the help of the hugest armed forces and the most sophisticated missile defence systems, for example – but required pro-active, or 'pre-emptive' as it was called at the time, actions abroad. (This was not exactly new; but it was a shock to realise that the fall of communism had not removed this kind of necessity.) Actual and potential enemies had to be pursued to *their* homelands: which was of course the main public rationale for the US (and British) onslaughts on Afghanistan and Iraq. But that was just a short-term solution. As well as this the Neocons believed – and Bush came to accept – that the world needed to be changed fundamentally politically, in order to do away with the conditions that were supposed to breed what Bush characterised as 'resentment and hatred' (towards America), or – another favourite word of his – 'evil'; which were, according to him, 'tyranny' and non-freedom abroad; starting with the Middle East, where most of the 'evil' had its origin. So, 'the survival of liberty in our land increasingly depends on the success of liberty in other lands', as he put it in his 2005 Inaugural Address; which was the *defensive* argument for trying to change other nations, by military means if all others failed, it was implied – or even if not. Needless to say, it was also bound to be to those other nations' benefit, which squared it with the Americans' idealism too. But it was probably the appeal to their domestic fears that persuaded the latter to accept it. (The Bush 2004 re-election campaign used TV images of wolves emerging threateningly from dark forests to underline the point.) To make her own people safe, America had to revolutionise the world.

This was not an entirely new ambition, any more than the more static 'shining city' one was; though it is probably oversimplifying things to say – as Robert Kagan does – that in taking it up now America was not really changing, but 'only became more itself'. This is to pick just one strand of American history and in the American 'national' character out of the several that are available, and exaggerate it beyond what would have appeared reasonable if the events of the early 2000s had not happened; very few nations are so straightforward and homogeneous in their cultures as to allow this, though nationalist and imperialist writers – compare Seeley – are fond of doing it. Nonetheless, there are precedents. The brief period of overt American imperialism in the 1890s, for example, threw up a number; including President McKinley, who justified his own administration's imperialism on the grounds that it would bring 'liberty . . .

floating over it'; Woodrow Wilson – the self-styled anti-imperialist of 1918 – who approved of the way it would enable the spread of American 'commerce and ideas' among the 'backward' races of the earth; and the famously enthusiastic Senator Albert J. Beveridge of Indiana, who thought that America's conquest of the Philippines was a sign that 'Almighty God' – no less – 'has marked us as His chosen people, henceforth to lead in the regeneration of the world.' So the idea of America's world-crusading mission had a pedigree.

This was the strand the Neocons took up in the 1990s (well before 9/11), when they insisted openly on the need for active American world domination – in most people's eyes 'imperialism', though the Neocons preferred expressions like 'expansive internationalism' for it – as the only way of achieving global 'liberty', and hence security for the USA. That sprang from the new (or new-ish) idea that 'democracies' could never, by their nature, go to war with one another, which meant that a 'free' world would be a peaceful one also. Some of these people, incidentally – including their long-dead guru Leo Strauss, a German originally, who had been attracted to the 'shining city' in the 1930s while on the run from Hitler's anti-Semitism, but who never really took to American culture – were far from truly *democratic* in their ideologies, except in so far as they thought the democracy could be harnessed to the cause of a greater America. Strauss also thought war would be intrinsically a good thing for the US, in order to toughen up a people 'feminised' by too much democracy (so he wouldn't have looked forward to the final pacific end of all this that his disciples were preaching now). There are resonances here of fascism. (Fascism: 'a form of political behaviour marked by obsessive preoccupation with community decline, humiliation or victimhood and by compensatory cults of unity, energy and purity': Robert Paxton.) For students of the old British Empire these men also bear a striking resemblance, in most aspects of their thinking, to the more extreme (proto-fascist) imperial ideologues of early twentieth-century Britain. (Many of these had been foreign-born, too.) One difference, however, is that in America in the early 2000s they came closer to real power.

The same *may* be true of another apparently important ideological influence in America at this time, which was religion: more specifically, the Evangelical Christian kind. The theologian Michael Northcott attributes Bush's own sense of world mission (once it had been nudged by 9/11) to this: his idea that America was *divinely* ordained not only to be an example to other lands (the original Puritan stance), but also the instrument for directly bringing 'liberty' to them. Thus, writes Northcott,

> Instead of a refuge from the storm, America becomes the storm, threatening to visit its military might, and its unchallenged supremacy as the sole remaining superpower, on those who would resist its influence: the 'enemies of freedom'. . . . The struggle to achieve this vision at home and overseas will require courage and perseverance but ultimately it will be successful because it is 'the angel of God who directs the storm'.

That, of course, fitted in with Bush's easy Manichaean talk of 'Good' and 'Evil' in the world, and of 'crusades': an unfortunate choice of a word in the context of a struggle with a part of Islam. And, according to Northcott, there was more.

In particular, there was 'premillennial dispensationalism': a theology supposedly shared by many millions of Americans, especially in the middle and southern states, which gave a very distinctive edge to their 'imperialism'. Premillennial dispensationalists believed that (hold on to your hats) they were God's chosen people, that He was directing them to save the whole world, that this was all predicted in the Bible, especially the sinfulness, wars and natural disasters of the present time; but not to worry about any of this, because it was just the prologue to the 'last dispensation': the seventh and last stage of human history foretold in the Book of Revelations, dominated by the Antichrist ruling through either the United Nations or the European Union (the Good Book was unclear on this); during which however the whole of Palestine would be returned to the Israelites, Solomon's temple would be rebuilt in Jerusalem (just where the Al-Aqsa mosque happened to be then), the Jews would convert to Christianity, and a thing called a 'Rapture' would magically pluck the faithful (mostly Americans, one presumes) up to heaven to escape this time of 'Great Tribulation', to be plonked down again when the thousand-year Reign of the Saints was inaugurated – and all quite soon. So that was something to look forward to. Much followed from this. There was no point in trying to make things better for people here on earth, for example – social reform, environmental protection – because that would take the edge off the Tribulation, and so slow things down. Peace between Israel and Palestine – ditto. Internationalism was just a cunning disguise for the reign of the Prince of Darkness. American impe-rialism was the agency of God's salvation. George W. Bush *himself* was the Angel of the Lord. Gosh.

How seriously was all this to be taken? It is of course the aspect of modern American life and politics that is most difficult for non-Americans (except Muslim fundamentalists, presumably) even to comprehend. (The more liberal half of America finds it hard too.) For a non-believer, reading Hal Lindsey's *The Late Great Planet Earth* (1970), a prime source for all this stuff, can be a disorientating experience. (When I came to his quite detailed description of the reign of Satan – a.k.a. the UN or the EU – I'm afraid the image that sprang to my mind first was that of the current US administration. That just shows how our perceptions can be shaped by our prejudices. But believers might like to check it out.) It is often dismissed for that reason. Yet we know that the 'Christian Right' was a crucial constituency for Bush, though it voted for him mainly on issues of personal 'morality', not foreign policy. Was Bush himself a premillennial dispensationalist? If so he didn't say, presumably for fear of scaring sensible voters (and Palestinians) off. If he was, it could have frightening implications, especially for those of us who aren't 'Chosen' (or haven't yet been told we are). It would explain some aspects of his policy in the Middle East, especially *vis-à-vis* Israel. It suggests a *form* of 'imperialism' that is far more grandiose than any ever envisioned by any nation in history before. It also points up another stark departure from the British precedent. Victorian Britain had her religious crazies too, but they were marginal in this context. Most practical British imperialists – even Gladstone, the invader of Egypt, who was probably the most religi*ose* of Britain's prime ministers – had their feet planted firmly on the ground. Hopefully the Americans who matter – the people who implement policy – have too. But it may be dangerous to underestimate the *slight* influence, at any rate, of madness (delusion, paranoia, etc.) in American politics generally, and US foreign policy in particular. It has seized other great nations, after all. There is no reason to think that America, just because she is 'modern', is immune.

Even discounting the 'madness', however, the sheer scale and simplicity of this set of ideas – what we might call its 'ideologism' – are extraordinary. British imperialists, apart from that brief Indian pre-1857 phase, and on the outer fringes of 1900s politics, had never been like this. British foreign policy-*makers* had generally been more pragmatic men; usually aristocratic, of course; wise in the ways of the world – over-wise, the ideologists might say; and antipathetic – even allergic – to what at that time was widely stigmatised as 'enthusiasm' – burning faith, simpleminded conviction, the 'crusading' impulse. They were the Anglicans of the imperial world. (The Church of England has usually in its history been a 'broad', tolerant faith. You didn't have to *believe* much to be part of it.) In more modern times, this kind of 'ideologism' was usually associated in Britain with extreme left-wing causes, especially communism – which was why the Soviet Union was so feared. Modern American *historicism* in particular recalls this powerfully; the astounding idea – not confined to the Neocons, but shared as we have seen by Albright and Clinton – that you knew for certain where 'history' was inevitably (the communists would say 'scientifically') headed; that you had unlocked *this* mystery, at any rate, of the universe; and, more than this, that you (America) represented this tendency yourself, which is what of course qualified you to impose it on others – this had always been the great *Marxist* idea before then. This is the major difference between British and American imperialisms, the shot of electricity that broke the latter free from the ordinary earthly trammels that had bound the former, and even – in practical terms – the latter, until this point. We need to be fully aware of this, as well as of the 'parallels'. The Neocon form of 'imperialism' was not *just* a continuation or repeat of the British. It transcended it.

Exceptionalism

The reasons for this incredible confidence, or hubris, have been much debated: by its critics, that is; for those who share it, they are obvious. We have alluded to one briefly already: America's sense of 'exceptionalism', or uniqueness and superiority compared with all other nations, which was, of course, one of the factors making it difficult for her to take on board any precedents for her current foreign policy at all. This is a fairly well-known attribute of many Americans at all times, an essential boost to their patriotism, or 'nationalism' as Anatol Lieven for example prefers to call it; based partly on the truly distinctive ideals on which they were formally founded as a nation, and partly on their widespread ignorance of other countries. It is taught explicitly in many – perhaps most – American schools, usually as part of a national 'history' that is fully as national*istic*, and, to outside observers, biased, as the histories taught in many totalitarian countries, and far more so than ever in imperial Britain. The idea itself of course goes back to the Puritans, and is one of a number of direct British contributions to the phenomenon. John Winthrop, of 'Citty upon a Hill' fame, was born in Suffolk (England). Most American ideas of 'liberty' also originated in Britain; and in fact continued there, as we saw (in Chapter 2), though Americans sometimes lost touch with this. This is the crucial factor, the one establishing the 'exceptionalist' myth. It's easy to see how it arose: the first white Americans were a long way from Europe, which when they had left it had been in a pretty tyrannous state; they had no need of Europe thereafter, except to replenish them with immigrants; and they had their time too cut out cultivating (and colonising) their own great new continent to be able to keep a check on the way the rest of the world was going. This was aggravated by their deliberate diplomatic 'isolationism' later on. Hence America's sense of 'difference' today. It is certainly not peculiar to her, but may have more serious repercussions in the case of a democratic hegemon. (Britons are probably just as ignorant, but it doesn't matter so much, because Britain isn't so important; and it didn't matter when she *was* important, because most of them didn't have the vote then.)

Everyone – every curled-lipped European, at any rate – knows the evidence for this supposed insularity. One of course is the minimal coverage of foreign affairs in the American press and on TV, unless US troops are fighting there. (It is the nineteenth-century American satirist Ambrose Bierce who is usually credited with the suggestion that 'war is God's way of teaching the Americans geography'.) Others cite the small proportion of Americans who even have passports (20 per cent?), though that is obviously unfair: North America is a big and varied enough place to satisfy most travellers; for many

Europeans foreign countries are only a short hop away; and how many of *them* would have passports if they only needed them to travel beyond their own continent? Slightly more worrying may have been George W. Bush's parochialism, if the widespread rumour was true (it may not have been) that he had only travelled abroad twice before he became President, both times to Mexico. Most Europeans who have lived in the USA can add to this stock of accounts of American parochialism. (My own contributions are the redneck who, when told by one of my students in upstate New York in the early 1970s that he was taking my course in British history, asked 'Why British history? America has the best history in the world'; and the remark I *think* I caught from a political commentator during CNN's coverage of the 2000 Presidential election that, muddy as that seemed to be, it still proved America's superiority, because 'in any other country of the world' – *any* other country – 'one of the candidates would have been taken out and shot'.)

With this kind of attitude (and I have met it at many different levels of American society, including academia) it is clearly difficult for some Americans to credit that anyone else might have anything at all to teach them; or even that there might be societies and systems out there that are different from theirs, but equally worthy of respect. This is a matter for concern. It does nobody good to think he's better than everyone else, whether or not he really is: which is always, of course, arguable. This is especially so when he is (or thinks he is) strong. It is likely to make him arrogant, cut him off from the experience of others, deprive him of empathy and even wisdom, and make him unwilling to cooperate with others: all characteristics that its critics believe they can discern in the attitudes and policies of the American administration today. It is this mind-set that produces *dicta* like the one we have already quoted from Condoleezza Rice, that 'American values are universal'. Imagine that being said about any other country. 'British values are universal.' It just doesn't work.

Of course, all this professed idealism may have been merely a cover for 'lower' and (for the more worldly wise, or cynical) more comprehensible *levels* of motivation, such as capitalist exploitation. Oil is the obvious suspect here. It is well known that America was more dependent on foreign oil than any other country in the world; had the most aggressive oil companies; and, at this time, had an administration – especially the President and Vice-President – which was soaked in the stuff. Iraq's massive and underexploited oil deposits were an obvious attraction. If the way to discover the motive for an event is to ask '*cui bono*?', the oil men leap into the frame immediately. Their ambitions were quite open; it's not as though you need to be ultra-suspicious to suspect them. 'There is no need for conspiracy theories,' writes one authority; 'never has a conspiracy been less interested in concealment.' Oil was a more *rational* reason for invading Iraq than speeding up the Second Coming. It is also a more normal kind of motive for 'imperialism', one that those of us schooled in other imperialisms are able to recognise easily. It is certainly something that American 'imperialism' has in common with British. After all that religious craziness and ideologism, simple greed like this comes almost as a relief.

Enmired in Iraq

It is never easy being a 'liberal imperialist'; which is probably the phrase from the old British imperial vocabulary that best approximates to what the Americans had become by the early 2000s, by their own best lights. (Actually, 'liberal imperialist' seems rather mild for it. 'Utopian imperialist' may be better.) It is especially difficult if you have had little practical experience of this kind of thing before, and have no real stomach for the 'ruling' part of it. That, of course, was America's situation after 2001. It was not of her choosing, though she had only herself to blame. There can be little doubt that she genuinely did not hanker after a territorial empire in the Middle East, just as her leaders claimed; it was what in their view made them *not* imperialists. Some new American military bases, yes, and hopefully some compliant rulers; but then they were likely to be compliant in any case, in gratitude for America's 'liberation' of their countries. This seems to have been the general idea: the US would go in and liberate Afghanistan and Iraq, and then after a brief hiatus those countries would start ruling themselves. 'You open it to the people and you begin a dialogue with the people,' Jay Garner, the first American administrator in Iraq, told a BBC interviewer shortly after his appointment. 'As you do that, the leaders will emerge and I think they'll take charge.' That, believed many American strategists, would then trigger off a general movement of democratisation in the Middle East, as others – ordinary Syrians, Egyptians, Iranians and so on – saw what it was doing for their neighbours. It was as easy as this. By all accounts, there was almost no prewar US planning beyond that for the administration of Afghanistan and Iraq after the wars. There didn't need to be. Iraqi exiles advising the administration told it that the American tanks that rolled into Baghdad after the end of the war there would be met by happy girls throwing sweets and flowers. 'We will be greeted as liberators,' the Vice-President assured a television audience four days before the invasion began. Democracy would automatically follow. That was the plan.

Again notoriously, that didn't happen; or at any rate not immediately. America and her allies were forced to stay behind in Afghanistan and Iraq longer than they had planned originally, coping with a resistance that theoretically should have melted away. Their agenda was clear: to establish (friendly) democracies – the 'liberal-imperialist' project; but it was proving more difficult to implement than almost anyone had anticipated. It was here that America's real troubles started. The invasions had gone swimmingly. US military power was such that it overwhelmed both the Afghan and the Iraqi conventional forces (without WMDs, of course) in weeks, and with very little loss of American lives: mainly because most of it was carried out through bombing from a safe height – the method pioneered by Britain in her colonies. On 1 May 2003 President Bush famously announced 'victory' in Iraq on the deck of the USS *Abraham Lincoln*, under a banner inscribed 'Mission Accomplished'. But that was clearly premature. America's problems were only just beginning. Sensibly, from their point of view – wickedly from most others – the Afghan and Iraqi resistances, with no chance against the Americans' military hardware, turned to other methods of attacking them and those they saw as their collaborators – police recruits, for example – which bypassed it. (A name for this is 'asymmetrical'.) Some of these were taken from the familiar techniques of guerrilla warfare, but with suicide bombings, kidnappings and executions (of any 'Westerners') now added to them, with deadly and terrifying effect. All this was ostensibly to liberate Afghanistan and Iraq from what the resisters, at any rate, regarded as US 'imperialism'.

These campaigns certainly bore a very close resemblance to many *anti*-imperialist movements of the past, for example in Ireland, Algeria, Kenya and Vietnam. Almost as significantly: the American authorities reacted to them in exactly the same ways. The demonisation of suicide bombers, for example; claims that the resistance represented only a small minority of the natives; that many of them were foreign adventurers; that they simply scared more 'moderate' natives into submission to them; that they represented something atavistic and primitive in the human psyche, or 'medieval' in the case of Islam; even Bush's common characterisation of them as 'evil' (a favourite word, this, when you are confronting something you don't understand): all are to be found in the counter-insurgency propaganda of past colonial powers, whether there is any truth in any of them or not. (There is some.) From this viewpoint the US had clearly got herself into a colonial-*type* situation now in these countries, whatever her original intentions had been. 'Although the United States has not created an empire in any formal sense,' writes Andrew Bacevich, 'it has most definitely acquired a colonial problem.' All could agree on that. This could be seen to lie at the root of her difficulty. Anxious not to appear too obviously 'imperialist', in denial about her imperial past and with no memories, it seemed, of the practical colonial experience she must have gained in, for example, the Philippines (very few Filipino pro-consuls would have been still alive then), she had no solid tradition of imperial governance to fall back on. All she had were her military strength, which had got her into this situation; and her ideals, which were supposed to get her out of it.

Sheer military force is a notoriously crude instrument for any sort of civil administration, rarely completely effective even on its own terms against peoples who have learned to circumvent its strengths and exploit its weaknesses, and more likely to provoke resistance than otherwise. The American military at this time appeared particularly 'crude': over-reliant on bombing (Falluja, for example, reduced to rubble in pursuit of dissidents in April 2004), trigger-happy, and seemingly unconcerned about innocent Iraqi victims, who were never, for example, officially counted. Then, of course, there were the notorious and appalling scandals that emerged from the prisons in which she detained suspected 'terrorists', administered by the US Army, in Guantanamo Bay (Cuba), Abu Ghraib (Iraq), and elsewhere. Much of this was clearly counter-productive, intensifying local hostility to the occupation and, in the eyes of many commentators, even breeding exactly those conditions, favourable to anti-American jihadism, it had ostensibly been supposed to neutralise. Al-Qaeda, for example, previously excluded from Iraq by its secular dictator, now had a new fertile field in which to recruit. In other words, America was making the problem (for herself) worse.

There were three broad reasons for this. The first is an obvious one: armies and air forces tend to behave like this anyway; violence is after all their main function, and one of their attractions for recruits. Beyond that, however, there may have been special *cultural* factors at work in the American case. Everyone is aware of the reputation, at least, of the USA as a particularly violent domestic society: the murder rates, death penalty, gun ownership, brutal prison regimes, shocking racism, violent Hollywood movies, and so on. Those acquainted with American history will also know of the terrific part played by war in that. It was suggested in the last chapter, tentatively, that this may have had something to do with her past experience as a colonialist society: with the rough culture of the most brutal kind of imperialism (settlement) being more reflected in the mainstream of *her* popular culture, through the 'Western' genre of novels and movies, than for example in Britain's case. America was *closer* to her imperialism than Britain ever was to hers. But there are other contributory factors too. Some people saw a precedent for Abu Ghraib in the tough conditions of America's own (massively populated) jails. The widespread culture of 'masculinism' in the US is a likely factor. Ignorance is another. Thirdly: such conduct seems to be a natural concomitant of colonialism, or of colonial-like policies, in certain situations. 'I did not realize', writes David Rieff – who had previously seen these two as alternatives – 'the extent to which imperialism is or at least can always become barbarism.' The most cursory reading of British colonial history illustrates that. Nothing coming from Abu Ghraib, for example, exceeded in horror certain crimes that were perpetrated under the British in post-Mutiny India, or in 1950s Kenya. Even the tortures and obscenities were there. This sort of thing is a likely – if not inevitable – side-effect of colonialism. This should give pause to those who wish to encourage the United States today to become more of an 'empire' in Britain's earlier mould. Along with the 'jodhpurs and pith helmets' (Max Boot: see the Introduction) can come *this*.

The problem with ideals

The other mainstay of American 'liberal imperialism', idealism, may have been equally untrustworthy. One fundamental law of imperialism (and maybe of all human endeavour) is that good intentions do not guarantee favourable results. Indeed, it is arguable that many of the worst evils in the history of the world have stemmed from these, more than – for example – greed for oil. 'God save us always', says Fowler in Graham Greene's *The Quiet American* (1955), set in French Indo-China, 'from the innocent and the good.' That is the other main drawback of idealism: that it is so often 'innocent' – that is, naïve, abstract, unschooled in the ways of the world, and too sure of itself. 'I've been in India, Pyle,' Fowler goes on – Pyle is the idealistic American CIA man whose best intentions cause so much havoc in the novel – 'and I know the harm liberals do.' The world is not always as simple a place as it may appear from the vantage point of the City on the Hill.

Of course Fowler could have been wrong. He is portrayed by Greene as a cynical amoralist, a typical 'old European' as Donald Rumsfeld would undoubtedly have regarded him ('Old Europe' was how Rumsfeld dismissed those countries who opposed the US invasion of Iraq in 2003), and not altogether reliable. It is too easy, and cheap, for Europeans to paint America as 'naïve' – the 'brash young nation' thing. (In fact the USA is considerably older as a nation than most modern European ones.) The British colonial experience, in India or anywhere else, is certainly not conclusive. Not many historians now would attribute the failures of the *raj* in Fowler's time, such as they were, to excessive 'liberalism'. (Before 1857, possibly.) Maybe if the British had been *more* idealistic in their colonial practice, as opposed to their rhetoric, than we have seen they were – more 'innocent', even – better might have come of it. It is impossible to say for sure. This may (2005) be about to be tested in Afghanistan and Iraq: if the Americans are true to *their* rhetoric, and persevere with the fast-track 'nation building' they began in 2001 and 2003. It could all work out, in spite of the suicide bombs, eventually.

Whatever the truth of this, however – and this book will be making no predictions – there are surely some lessons the Americans might have learned from the Europeans' (and their own) past imperial experiences, if only they had been prepared to admit the parallels. It was their insistence that what they were doing then was completely new and different that landed them in what were, broadly speaking, the fine messes that were Afghanistan and Iraq immediately after 2001 and 2003. They thought their motives were better. They were bearing gifts: especially markets, and democracy. They didn't want to 'rule' the natives longer than necessary. Indeed, they instituted elections in both countries with almost indecent haste. There was much to commend in this vision. It paid the natives the compliment of assuming that they *could* rule themselves. (The British were rarely so charitable.) But it didn't work out, at least in the short term. Another of the reasons for this, apart from military excess, was the Americans' initial lack of sensitivity to a whole host of factors on the ground, including cultural differences, the relativity of 'values', and local national feeling. The examples of previous empires, including the British, could have alerted them to these. Britain had also started off, in some of her colonies, with many of these same naïvetés; but then learned her lesson the hard way. America, it seemed, would need to learn it all over again, painfully.

The question of 'values' is fundamental. Most other peoples – again, religious zealots and ideologists would need to be excluded – realise just how relative most of them are. Even if there *are* universal ones – the sanctity of human life, liberty, peace, and so on – they are so open to various interpretations, and clearly encrusted and distorted by local cultural influences, as to make any one version of them unreliable as a model for others. In America's case it is easy, for outsiders at any rate (and for many domestic critics), to see where these cultural influences have impacted. The dominant American perception of 'democracy' is one such area, whose subordination to certain other American discourses, like capitalism, can make it seem seriously deficient even by some 'democratic' yardsticks. Other peoples are understandably sceptical of it; 'partly', writes Michael Ignatieff, 'because of the chaos of the contested presidential election in 2000, which left the impression, worldwide, that closure had been achieved at the expense of justice. And partly because of the phenomenal influence of money on American elections'. Many Europeans believe their systems are *more* essentially democratic than the American; plausibly, I would say, in the case of Scandinavia. Yet despite this, Ignatieff goes on, 'Americans have difficulty understanding that there are many different forms that this yearning' – for freedom – 'can take. . . . Democracy may be a universal value, but democracies differ – mightily – on ultimate questions.'

On other issues too, the American 'model', viewed from the outside, might seem not the best one to follow. Its violent side, mentioned already, was the aspect most often cited; black ghetto communities living in poverty, revealed terribly to all the world in the wake of Hurricane Katrina that engulfed New Orleans in September 2005, was another. But there were other criticisms that were made of the American 'system' too. Even if that had been more ideal than it was, one could understand if foreigners sometimes failed to discern its virtues clearly through the fog of atrocious behaviour that America in the recent past had sometimes visited on *them*: anti-democratic plots, support for tyrants, murders of popular leaders – as I revise this chapter

Pat Robertson, a prominent leader of the American 'religious Right', is urging the assassination of a South American president who is hostile to US capitalism – and countless other smaller crimes, especially at the hands of her servicemen and women (though mainly the men) stationed in all those bases abroad. This isn't *of course* to say that America is necessarily 'worse' than other countries (for what it's worth, I believe my own country, Britain, is less 'democratic' than America in most ways); only that her own 'freedom', even her democracy, is not perfect (of course), and so maybe not good enough to be a 'model' for others. 'Cities on Hills' need to be more shining than this.

Away from 'democracy', another matter for concern was the 'values' usually *omitted* from the American list: such as peace, social justice, gender equality, and the human right to food and shelter. (On the gender question, it is interesting that Bush mainly talked about spreading 'respect' – not 'equality' – for women: a formulation that of course implies that men are the subject of this – you don't need to ask women to respect women; is so vague as to allow almost anything – Victorian men 'respected' women by not subjecting their angelic natures to the crudities of political activity, for example; and was also phrased, incidentally, precisely the form of words that British imperialists used to justify the superiority of *their* 'civilisation' over Islam and others.) None of this is to say that these values necessarily *are* as 'universal' as the Americans' (though as it happens I personally believe they are); only that they would seem to have at least as much right as the latter to be considered as such. Nor, again, is this intended as a critique of America *in particular*. The point being made here – an obvious one, surely – is that *every* society is like this; that if there *is* a kind of Platonic ideal of human social and political conduct in the world – this is before considering the possibility that there might not be, the absolute moral relativist view – it is never to be found *unen-crusted*; and that consequently a nation in the situation America finds herself in then should be careful not to confuse *its* ways with what may be best for everyone. There were signs a couple of years into the Iraq occupation that the American government was beginning to catch on to this. 'When the soul of a nation finally speaks,' said Bush, somewhat portentously, in his 2005 Inaugural Address, 'the institutions that arise may reflect customs and traditions very different from our own. America will not impose our own style of government on the unwilling.' That was obviously meant to reassure people on this point. (Perhaps it was also the reason for that 'respect for women' thing: even male chauvinist Muslims could sign up to that.) It was one of the first lessons most British imperialists, too, learned quite early on: the 'indirect rulers' and so on; cultural relativists – to an extent – to a man and a woman. This was one reason why they were able to hang on so long to their empire, in such small numbers; but also probably, it has to be said, why they were not more *effective* than we have seen they were, as what today would be called 'nation-builders'.

But then the British had always had a different way of looking at 'nation-building' generally. We have alluded to this already: their idea of the achievement of 'freedom' as a gradual process, rather than a one-off event. Of course this reflects the peculiarity of Britain's own history, with – as we saw in an earlier chapter – her liberties being perceived as developing slowly but solidly, in stages, tailored to contemporary customs and cultures, and usually unbloodily; *by contrast* with the dangerous revolutionary upheavals of other nations, which usually – they were thinking mainly of the French Revolution here, but the Russian came along later to confirm it – couldn't be relied upon to bring true freedom in any case. There is an interesting analogy to be drawn here from another field. Britain's experience of political progress made her 'evolutionary' in her thought about this; America's seems more 'creationist' – the miracle of 1776, and Bush's insistence that 'freedom' is divinely ordained. Britons generally saw it as a more 'natural' and 'human' development. It is this that inclined them more to gradualist policies in their colonies too; sometimes so gradualist as to be almost imperceptible – we have raised the obvious doubts about the genuineness of Britain's real commitment to even 'eventual' self-government here previously. By contrast, America wanted it done all at once: liberation – a constitution (Britain of course had *never* had one of those) – democracy; 1776–89 (or that miraculous week in 4004 BCE) all over again.

A further implication of this, of course, was supposed to be that America would not need an imperial cadre of men (and by now women, hopefully) to run her new and very temporary empire for her; which was just as well, because she did not have one. Of course America had ambassadors, military men and academics who could do the top jobs for her: the first post-invasion US ambassador to Afghanistan, for example, Robert P. Finn, was a Princeton professor in Middle Eastern Studies; and the first two American 'administrators' in Iraq, Jay Garner and Paul Bremer, were a retired general and a career diplomat respectively (the latter with a profitable sideline in insurance policies against terrorist attack for businesses). None of these, however, was schooled in *ruling*, or had the distinctive ruling values that had so marked British (and other European) colonial administrators in the past – the mistrust of capitalism, for example. The reason for this was quite fundamental; it arose from the structure and nature of America's society, and especially its more uniformly 'market' or 'capitalist' ethos, by contrast with nineteenth- and early twentieth-century Britain's more 'hybrid' one. 'Paternalists' cannot be bred to order. They need the right socio-economic conditions, and ideally a long tradition, to nurture them. It is difficult to imagine the modern democratic and capitalist US producing a proper ruling class of this kind. This is why America will almost certainly not be able to follow Niall Ferguson's well-meaning – but, one suspects, not very hopeful – advice in

Colossus (2004), and emulate the British Empire more closely. That may not necessarily be a bad thing. One thing about 'rulers', as we have seen, is that they tend to slow things down. But it had important implications for the Americans in Afghanistan and Iraq. It meant that their fast-track strategy, for bringing democracy quickly to these countries, had to work. Otherwise they had little to fall back on: except brute – and expensive – force.

Alternatives

It could work. This needs to be emphasised. There are British imperial precedents for much of what the US is doing today in the Middle East and elsewhere which don't on the face of it seem encouraging; but these are not conclusive. Precedents never are. History doesn't work like this. It never repeats itself exactly. Projects that are unsuccessful once can succeed the next time around. It is possible – though it is unnerving for a historian to think so – that they will stand more chance of succeeding if their authors are unaware of, and so unintimidated by, their failures in the past. This may all just be the jaded talk of 'Old Europe' – Graham Greene's unprincipled Fowler – in any case. The Pyles may be right. 'History' may really be 'marching on', as Condoleezza Rice puts it, 'towards markets and democracy'. The process may be unstoppable. If Britain's old-school paternalists had let her capitalists have their head more in the nineteenth century, it might have come to its culmination sooner. Then we wouldn't be in the hole we are in today. Of course, it requires a great leap of ideology to believe this: equivalent to, for example, the Counter-Reformation's faith in its God in the sixteenth century; the French Revolution's faith in the 'Enlightenment' project in the late eighteenth; the British Whig faith in the inevitability of 'progress' in the nineteenth century; and the communists' faith in their 'dialectic' in the early twentieth. (All these gave rise to 'imperialisms' of sorts.) But present-day capitalist ideology in America, in some of its manifestations at any rate, seems to be well up there with these: in terms of its *certainty*, for example. Maybe this time we really have found the Holy Grail. It was in the Shining City all the time. This isn't meant sarcastically. (Well, only a little.) The historian must be open to any possibility. This one just might be true.

If so, then the Americans (and their allies) would be relieved. The alternatives must have been worrying to them. One was that they remained stuck in Afghanistan and Iraq for years, even decades, rather like Britain became in Egypt, but at far greater cost, both in money and lives. This was what Niall Ferguson recommended. But there were considerable doubts (not least in his own mind) over whether the American people would stomach this – the 'body bags', for example; naturally, after the way they were supposed to have resiled against the war in Vietnam. There could also be a liberal reaction. One of the dangers J. A. Hobson always warned against in connection with imperialism was the way it tended to rebound on domestic freedoms: the 'empire strikes back' effect. His concern was mainly with the influence of 'Indian' – that is, autocratic *British* Indian – habits of rule back home. In America, with fewer pro-consuls but more generals, the concern was slightly different: for the *militarisation* of American politics and society, expressed, for example, in Andrew Bacevich's *The New American Militarism: How Americans are Seduced by War* in 2005. Measures like America's Homeland Security Act could possibly be seen in this 'empire strikes back' light too. One would expect Americans, however, with their proud libertarian traditions, to be especially resistant to that, just as the British were (Hobson's fears were not borne out); at least in the longer term. That boded ill for imperialists. Joseph Nye warned that America could 'rot from within' – presumably morally. That too echoes right-wing concerns in 1900s' Britain about the threat to their Empire from national 'deterioration' and the like. Other commentators worried whether the US – already running a huge national deficit – could afford all this. A lengthy occupation could also have a further repercussion: to make her weaker in other parts of the world, unable to act as freely and decisively as she might like against (for example) foreign powers who posed genuine nuclear threats, rather like nineteenth- and early twentieth-century Britain was weakened *vis-à-vis* the continent of Europe; because of what Paul Kennedy called 'imperial overstretch'. (For a few years after America's 'victory' in the Cold War Kennedy was derided over this phrase: but no longer. People are holding their breath again.)

A second possibility was chaos and anarchy: if America withdrew prematurely from Afghanistan and Iraq, and 'history' didn't march the way it was supposed to. A third was the free election in these countries of *un*grateful and *un*compliant governments, maybe even Islamic fundamentalist ones: what would the US do then? A fourth risk was a return to the old American line, of propping up unpleasant regimes simply because they *were* compliant, and were believed to be necessary to American security: the strategy that had led the US to support Saddam Hussein in the 1980s, for example, and Islam Karimov (Uzbekistan) as late as the early 2000s. Finally, an unsuccessful 'liberal imperialism' would almost certainly further alienate most of the rest of the world, already greatly miffed by America's assertive unilateralism not only in this field, but in others: a fate that did not seem to concern her much originally, when she snubbed the United Nations in 2003, for example; but which came to concern her later, in the age of 'overstretch', when she began to modify her rhetoric, at least, in order to rebuild international friendships. All these unfavourable outcomes would be avoided, of course, if the ideologues were proved right. It would be wonderful thing if so; not least, the sight of all those anti-imperialists and Old Europeans eating humble pie.

American imperialism

Was this 'imperialism'? The consistent line taken in the present book has been that this question doesn't really matter. It is interesting, enlightening and maybe even in some ways useful to compare modern American foreign policy with past imperialisms; but not simply in order to categorise it, or give it a name. Almost every imperialism in history has been in a category of its own. It has shared characteristics with other imperialisms of course, but there are always distinctive traits. Most recent imperialists – British and Russian, for example – have preferred to emphasise the differences rather than the similarities, especially when some sort of odium is thought to attach to previous empires; many have maintained that the differences are so significant as not to qualify theirs as 'imperialism' at all. Modern America (or her government) was simply repeating this. That could be said to be something she had in common with past empires. But of course it wasn't enough to make her outlook 'imperialist' on its own.

Whatever it was, it was an extraordinary project. In some ways 'imperialism' seems too *small* a word for it. America's early twenty-first century 'hegemony' was already greater than that of any empire in history; though it is arguable that it was not as secure militarily as it might have been if she had not got her forces bogged down in Iraq, or as deep commercially or culturally as those ubiquitous golden McDonald's 'M's all over the world made it appear. More remarkable from the standpoint of imperial*ism* – that is, the deliberate *extension* of hegemony – was her vision; or rather, that of the ideologues who guided the second President George Bush: in any other political language, the 'imperial*ists*'. The idea that America could exert 'full spectrum dominance' over the entire world was awesome, and went far beyond anything dreamed of by previous empires. Even more impressive was the idea that America could be so certain of what both God and 'history' (or should that have an initial capital too?) intended for human beings, as to feel entitled to force it on them at the point of a sword (or a missile). To 'liberate' humankind, to bring all peoples to the 'End of History' in one sense or another (millenarian or capitalist), to shine upon the whole world: that really does go beyond 'imperialism' in any of the older, more modest meanings of the word. The British Empire – our comparator here – was never as hubristic as this.

Of course it can be deflated – reduced to a more ordinary imperial scale. Some aspects of the American vision can appear narrow to non-American eyes (or even, of course, critical American ones). We have suggested already that it is likely to have been formed more by the special circumstances of America at that time – her distinctive and often idiosyncratic culture – than by God, History, or any other more authoritative Creator; in other words, these were *merely* American values, not 'universal' ones. This changes the picture entirely. 'Enlightening' the world is one thing; forcing your particular ideas on it is quite another. The second looks more like a certain very familiar kind of imperialism than the first. But of course it is largely a matter of perception. One can see why Rumsfeld and Co. couldn't see it – if what to the rest of the world looked like an alien ideology was merely 'enlightenment' in their eyes. Which, as we have already admitted, it may just possibly be.

The second way of reducing American policy to a 'mere' imperialism is to cast doubt on all this idealism; not this time on its validity, but on its genuineness as a motive for American policy. It could all have been a pretence. America went into Iraq for oil, and to enrich her own oil companies, but clothed the whole sordid enterprise in the high-flown rhetoric of 'democracy', to make it look better. These questions are never easy to answer definitively. As has been suggested already, it's not just a question of 'evidence' and its interpretation, but of perspective – it depends from whose viewpoint you are looking. Imperialisms happen for a complex of reasons and motives. In South Africa in the 1890s, for example, you had gold capitalists, ideological imperialists, local politicians, naval strategists and even a few humanitarians all pushing for Britain to go to war against the Transvaal Republic; all these factors were probably instrumental in bringing the war on, *plus* a timely accident – the Boer ultimatim – which triggered it off. In Iraq, similarly, there was definitely an oil lobby pressing for war, but also this ideological one (the Neocons), and another timely accident: 9/11, and the Iraqi President's mishandling of the fall-out from that. In both these – British and American – cases you have the additional complication that many of the ideologues did not necessarily regard material interests as 'sordid' in any case: *vide* David Livingstone's bracketing of 'commerce and civilisation' in the nineteenth century, and then *cf.* Condoleezza Rice's talk of 'markets and democracy' 150 years later. The 'ideals' of a capitalist culture are different from those of others. So it's complicated. But then, so it was in most previous cases of 'imperialism', too.

Throughout her history, right from her beginnings as a nation, America has been an *expansionary* power, with 'expansion' being at least as important to her as the rather more celebrated ideal of 'liberty'. We can all probably agree on that. Sometimes that expansion has been peaceful – commercial, for example; but not always. Violence and war have also played a prominent and even a characteristic part in it, reflected, for example – to an extent they never were in Britain – in America's national culture. Add to that a powerful economic motive (oil, arms), a sense of mission (the City on the Hill), unprecedented military strength (full spectrum dominance), a well-placed imperialist faction (the Neocons again), a weak-minded President (George W.), and a panic about 'national security' (9/11), and you have the recipe for what in most contexts would be called 'imperialism' – or, if you like, 'liberal imperialism', or 'neo-imperialism', or one of Mark Steyn's more 'wussified

Clinto-Blairite' terms for it. The main difference in the modern American case, of course, is that she doesn't want to *rule* other countries directly. Of course she doesn't; ruling is a difficult, expensive and thankless business, as the British found; it also requires rul*ers*, which America doesn't have; and sits less comfortably with America's ideal, or myth, of 'liberty' than it managed to with Britain's. That is why America's 'hegemony' will probably never develop into an 'empire' on the British model – the only prediction I am going to risk in this book – whatever might be the theoretical (and they *are* only theoretical) benefits of that. Whether that makes her any the less 'imperialist' is *merely* a matter of semantics.

Despite this, there are certainly parallels that can be drawn with the old British Empire, and especially with its 'free trade' or 'informal' phase in the early and mid nineteenth century. Even here, however, there are huge differences. One is present-day America's military might; another is her ideological certainty. Britain never possessed either of these advantages (or whatever) to anything like the same degree. It is these factors, together with the 'ruling' thing, that most distinguish recent American foreign policy from British imperialism: not only in the latter's nineteenth- and early twentieth-century guise, when Britain had an empire; but also in the early twenty-first century, when she didn't any longer (apart from the Falklands), but became closely associated – incongruously in many ways – with George W. Bush's.

4

'Still a global player'
British post-imperialism

Britain was something else. By joining with America in her invasions of Afghanistan and Iraq she made it look as though she shared the same – imperial or whatever – vision with her. Her policy was also widely seen as a return to the British imperialism of fifty or a hundred years before. There may have been something in the latter view; but there was very little in the former. In fact, one of the interesting things about the new British 'imperialism' of the early 2000s is the way it exemplifies the differences between the two countries' imperial visions. This wasn't always immediately apparent, because of the way America dominated the alliance, drowning out Britain's smaller voice with her clamour. In many ways, however, America and Britain were rather uncomfortable bedfellows, despite the great show of loyalty, mutual admiration and even affection that was presented at this time between Bush and Britain's Labour Prime Minister Tony Blair.

Imperial remains

The links between the old British imperialism and the new are there, but possibly not quite so straightforwardly as some observers assume. There is a common idea, especially abroad, that Britain never shed her general 'imperialist' culture after decolonisation, but merely kept it hidden under the surface of things. It was well expressed by Martin Jacques, in a *Guardian* article of October 2002.

> Once an imperial nation, always an imperial nation, even when the substance of power has long since disappeared. It is a mentality, a way of being and thinking. As a nation we still have a desperate need to believe that we still matter. . . . Buried deep in the national psyche, in a way that affects each and every one of us, is a desperate desire to believe that we are the best: it is a part of our imperial genetic make-up, shared only by other imperial nations like the US and France.

So the devil had never been properly exorcised. That was what they were espying looming out of the shadows now. This complements another widespread view of Britain, again particularly abroad, as an ex-imperial power struggling to come to terms with her 'decline'; having 'lost an empire and not yet found a role', as former American Secretary of State Dean Acheson famously put it in 1962 – with the clear implication that she continued hankering after her old imperial ermine, quite pathetically, for years afterwards. Hence Prince Harry, perhaps. (In January 2005 pictures of the third in line to the British throne at a fancy-dress party were splashed over the tabloid newspapers. The theme was 'Colonials and Natives'. Did that indicate nostalgia? Harry himself was wearing a Nazi uniform, whose relevance to the main theme seems puzzling, unless he was making a strikingly anti-imperialist point. More likely is that he just thought it was a bit of fun.) This is an important idea, because it is taken to be a major explanation for many other features of late twentieth-century British society, especially negative ones, like racism and Europhobia. In fact, in so far as it is supposed to refer to the British people *generally* ('as a nation'), it is almost certainly false.

One of the roots of it may be the assumption that 'imperialism' was *ever* a 'big deal' for the British people as a whole – outside, that is, the Prince's shallow set. If it had been, then they *must* have missed it. But it wasn't, as we saw in Chapter 1. So they didn't. All the evidence points this way. Popular ignorance of the Empire is one piece. A survey of public opinion carried out for the Colonial Office in 1948 revealed that most people did not know what a (dependent) colony was; only 49 per cent could name a single one correctly (3 per cent named America; one suggested 'Lincolnshire'); and – perhaps most revealingly – those who knew most about the Empire were also the most likely to disapprove. Nearly everyone at the time applauded India's and Pakistan's liberation, and then at least tolerated the other stages of decolonisation when they came. There were no great political ructions caused by the process, as in France; no governments thrown out, for example. The only possible exception is the Suez fiasco of 1956, when Britain tried vainly to reassert some of her old imperial control in Egypt; but that was the cause of the downfall of only one (ill) prime minister, and the action was widely unpopular in the country. Otherwise the Empire was dismantled with hardly a flutter of protest, apart from Enoch Powell (see Chapter 1), some older Tory buffers (Powell was a surprisingly young buffer), and the ridiculous little 'League of Empire Loyalists'. So far as racism and Europhobia are concerned, there are clearly other and more plausible explanations for both. The 'mass' immigration of the 1950s onwards is one. You obviously don't need to have had an empire to experience these things. Denmark also has racism, and Sweden Europhobia (Swedes also have a huge sense that they are 'the best', *pace* Jacques); neither, however, had been an imperial power recently – unless you count Greenland and the worldwide hegemony in the pre-packed furniture market of IKEA.

In fact the Empire was all but forgotten (or perhaps suppressed) in Britain in the immediate post-Empire age. It was scarcely ever taught in schools and universities, for example, to the annoyance both of those who still believed it was worth celebrating – later they attributed the neglect to 'political correctness' – and of those who thought it was shameful, but felt that young Britons should be told that their country could be appalling too. (It wasn't only the Germans.) I remember learning nothing about the Empire at my school, for example, or at university, where the only imperial history subject on offer (it was called, tellingly, 'The Expansion of Europe') was widely regarded as only for those who weren't up to the alternative 'History of Political Thought' course. In fact, however, as we have seen, that situation wasn't terribly new; even at its height the Empire had tended to be downplayed in British education. Politically 'imperialism' took on almost wholly negative connotations in the postwar period, owing partly to the influence of Marxist and other left-wing thinking at that time. To say that it was 'unfashionable' is to understate the case. Imperialists were ridiculed: quite literally; 'Major Bloodnok' in the 1950s radio comedy series *The Goon Show* is an example. Occasionally one would poke his head above the parapet – 'not a bad thing, the jolly old Empire' – only to be met by a fusillade from the vigilant antis. Usually they wisely lay low. How many of these there were, under the surface of Britain's new, modern, post-imperial society, it is impossible to tell. It probably wasn't a large number; and if most of them were ex-colonial servants, their ranks will have been thinning every year. *These* probably do not constitute the link between the two imperialisms (early and late). That needed a *revival* of interest in the British Empire, by a postcolonial generation – one that had not been around, or adult, when for example the horrors of the late colonial conflicts in Cyprus or Malaya or Kenya were going on – to refresh people's images of their Empire; or, in effect, to reimagine it.

This started happening around the 1980s. The roots of it are complicated. It was partly a reaction – justified in my view –

to the excesses of the anti-imperialism of the past. The British Empire, as I tried to show in the first main chapter of this book, was a complex phenomenon, and not best understood as simply exploitation, or a massive crime. The new light in which it began to be seen also owed something to the more general political reaction that Margaret Thatcher either set in motion, or (more likely) rode, when she came to power in 1979; when it suddenly became respectable again to praise 'capitalism', for example, and 'patriotism', and 'discipline' – and 'empire'. This was exhilarating for the Right. All these notions had used to be traduced by 'socialism', which for Thatcher, as for her great friend Ronald Reagan, was the number one enemy. Thirdly, there was a revival of imperial nostalgia, especially in films and TV drama serials set in British India; which, however fair they tried to be to both (or all) sides there, inevitably created a sense of imperial splendour which will have been new to many in their audiences, and seemed attractive. One or two academic historians followed on, with popular books and in one case a TV series self-consciously trying to rehabilitate the Empire: that is, to present it as *on balance*, at any rate, a 'good thing'. They were usually Thatcherites, incidentally, and not imperial historians originally. Most of the latter were critical of them; a fact that unfortunately did not register with many of their foreign readers, especially, who took them to be typical of the endemic imperialism they had always suspected – or wished to believe – lay under the surface of British society. And so the myth was prolonged.

All that however is about the British *people*, who really had little to do with the subject of this chapter – even less than the American people had to do with the subject of the last. It was not they who dragged their imperial ermine behind them into the later twentieth century, but their leaders (and the Prince). Several of these, prime ministers especially, exhibited signs – possibly delusions – of grandeur which can be attributed to that. It took some time for those who presided over the demise of the formal Empire, for example, to realise that they couldn't still hang on to some kind of worldwide economic and strategic control for decades to come – perhaps for ever – 'informally'. Much of their early diplomacy was directed to that. Britain's (thermo-nuclear) 'Bomb' was also thought to be a factor, a kind of Joker in the pack when it came to the relative strengths of nations: for what did it matter if Britain could not afford the legions to compete with the USA and USSR, if she still had the capacity to take out their capital cities with a single blow? These illusions faded around the mid-1960s, however, when Harold Wilson's Labour government was finally forced to withdraw militarily 'east of Suez' (or, by another way of looking at it, chickened out). This didn't mean that Britain's imperial past had ceased to exert a pull on prime ministers. But from the 1960s onwards it manifested itself in different ways: in a belief that Britain could still exert 'leadership', even without her legions; and in the idea that her imperial experience made her uniquely wise in the ways of the world.

Looking back on it from today, much of this can appear rather pathetic: Harold Macmillan's image of himself as a wise old uncle to the vigorous young President Kennedy, for example (that was much derided at the time, for instance in a famous sketch in the satirical stage review *Beyond the Fringe*); Harold Wilson's idea that Britain was uniquely placed to bring the war in Vietnam to an end; Margaret Thatcher's embarrassing bombast in Europe; the idea – the *very* idea – that it was John Major who stiffened the first President Bush's backbone over Kuwait in 1991; and so on. Most hostile observers, especially (again) abroad, saw more than a smidgeon of post-imperial posturing in all this. Thatcher was the prime suspect here, of course, in view of the war she pursued in 1982 actually over a remnant of the British Empire (the Falkland Islands): how much more proof did you need? In fact Thatcher is a problematical figure in this context. The Falklands War can obviously be defended on other than 'imperialist' grounds: resistance to aggression by a military dictator, for one. Logically Thatcher ought not to have been an imperialist in the 'formal' sense of the word, with her strong 'free market' beliefs, and the essential involvement in the old Empire of the 'paternalistic' classes she so much despised. But she probably didn't know enough imperial history to be aware of this. What she was, was a British patriot, with a strong awareness of Britain's past 'greatness'; which she attributed mainly to its non-socialism – she was obsessed with 'socialism' – but for which she sometimes cited the Empire as evidence of. All these prime ministers (even the socialist Wilson) had a similar view of Britain's underlying 'greatness' which was partly, at least, derived from her imperial past. You don't find other leaders of medium-sized nations throwing their weight about in the world in these kinds of way.

The Empire could also, however, impinge in other ways. Britain might take a *moral* dividend from her colonial past (as it was perceived). 'Britain is no longer the equal of the US or Russia in material resources and capacity for war,' wrote Lord Hailey as early as 1944, 'but she can still be the greatest of all countries in helping smaller and more backward peoples towards greater abundance and freedom under law in a world at peace.' The ideal vehicle for this kind of role was thought to be the British Commonwealth. The Commonwealth, remember, was not an Empire-substitute (those who hoped it might be were soon disabused), but something a good deal more idealistic; or, to put it differently, a distillation of the idealistic *aspects* of the old imperialism. The crucial development here was the voluntary adhesion to it in 1947 of newly independent India, which broke through the racial barrier to membership (all the previous Dominions were 'white'), and warmed the cockles of many old imperialists' hearts. Most of Britain's other ex-colonies took the same course. This seemed to give some credence to the myth that we saw being sown in the interwar years, of the Empire itself as, in effect, nothing more sinister than a friendly extended family all along; one in which children were kept in the nest only to nurture them and prepare them for flight, after which they would always gratefully keep in touch with their elders. It justified Britain's claims that she had always regarded her imperial role as a (familial) 'trusteeship' one, and so didn't need to be told this by the Americans. It was why the issue of 'self-government versus independence' had been so very important to Britain's political leaders in the wartime discussions with America (see chapter 2). It also had the effect of making decolonisation appear more of a transformation than a loss to many contemporary Britons, which softened the blow.

For idealists, however, there were other points in its favour. It was not an association based on power. (That may be why it appeared invisible to some, especially in powerful states, which often seem blind to non-power relations.) Later it dropped the word 'British' entirely from its title, to emphasise its 'round table' character. It was self-consciously multi-ethnic, which was thought to be of immense potential value in a world where racism was coming to seem one of the great evils of the future. In this respect it held a clear advantage over the United States, whose own racial situation was – to say the least – problematical; and over the slightly later EEC (EU), the other main rival for Britain's affections, which at that time was almost totally made up of whites. So it was a *liberal* institution. Those who were most enthusiastic about it after 1947, in fact, were generally not the old, macho 'power politics' imperialists (Thatcher for example despised it), but the more liberal and utopian kind; together with many quite kosher *anti*-imperialists – including the present author. Naïve we may have been; but to have assisted in creating and developing an organisation which rejected the domination of one nation or race over others, and bypassed the whole 'power' way of thinking that goes with it, was not an ignoble role. The problem with it was not so much the thing itself – the

institution of the Commonwealth and the ideals it represented –
as the distorted image it gave of the Empire that had preceded it,
by its focusing *on* those idealistic aspects of it, and sweeping into
the background its seamier sides. It may have been this that aided
its rehabilitation later on.

New Labour and imperialism

In British politics and political ideology, 'imperialism' has at
least as good a Liberal/socialist pedigree as a Conservative one.
(One can say the same of American Democrats.) Literal conservatives aren't keen on changing or reforming too much at
home, let alone abroad; that's why they call themselves conservatives. As the third Marquis of Salisbury once put it, referring
specifically to foreign policy, 'Whatever happens will be for the
worse, and therefore it is in our interest that as little should
happen as possible.' Free marketist Conservatives – the more
radical kind – are against using the *state* to bring about reform.
That knocks away two crucial legs of most kinds of imperialism, especially the one that purports to be using the power of
one nation for the benefit of others. Liberals on the other hand,
if they are confident enough *in* their liberalism, are quite often
found eager to spread its benefits to others, if they – which
generally means their governments – have the means to do so.
Socialists in history have been no different. This is why so few
British Labour Party leaders of the earlier twentieth century
were unequivocally anti-imperialist; most of them only wanted
to put an end to the imperialism of capitalist exploitation (see
above, Chapter 1: references to Hobson). So it should have
come as no great surprise that the new Labour government that
was elected to power in Britain in 1997 should have exhibited
more signs of a 'liberal imperialist' mentality than any of the
very free marketist Conservative ones that had been in power
for eighteen years before then.

We must be careful here. It depends what we mean by 'imperialist'. By the end of the twentieth century that word was coming to be used far more broadly and, it could be said, loosely than fifty years before. We've mentioned this already (in the Introduction). In addition, Britain was particularly vulnerable to loose charges of 'imperialism' at this time, on account both of her past history and of the assumption – discussed in the last section – that she had not been able to get over it. So, if she criticised an African tyrant, for example, it was widely interpreted – not least by that tyrant – as a sign that Britain still had imperial designs on his nation; if she gave aid to a 'Third World' country it was taken as a symptom of post-imperial guilt, or else a subtle means of exerting postcolonial control. At the very least her attitudes were taken to be imperially 'patronising'. It was getting to be difficult for her to do anything at all in any part of the world in which she had formerly had a colonial interest – which was most of it outside Europe – without attracting some such obloquy. Even if much of it was unwarranted, this could be seen as a reason for Britain to leave these countries well alone. Her past record, thought one commentator, surely made her 'the last country on the planet' to be interfering in their affairs.

For a government that might want to interfere nonetheless, there were two ways of tackling this. One was to emphatically deny the charge. That was Foreign Secretary Jack Straw's strategy, when confronted by it in November 2002: 'I don't agree with that stuff. I'm not a liberal imperialist.' He then added for good measure – to prove his anti-imperialist credentials, perhaps – some stinging criticisms of Britain's past colonial record, which drew predictable protests from the old fogeys: 'The Foreign Secretary traduces the British Empire: surely this must be the last straw,' chaffed one *Daily Telegraph* letter-writer; as well as from the new academic school of Empire rehabilitationists. Straw's response can be compared to Bush and Rumsfeld's in America: 'we don't do empire' (any more). The second approach was very different. That was to take a leaf from the rehabilitationists' book, defend Britain's imperial record, and *almost* admit that you were carrying it on. Tony Blair for example is supposed to have planned to mention the Empire favourably in a speech in Manchester during the general election campaign of 1997, until persuaded to cut it at the last moment by some of his horrified colleagues. Gordon Brown, his Chancellor, was less coy, openly admitting to his own 'pride' in the Empire in January 2005, and expressing the view that the time had now come for Britons to cease endlessly 'apologising' for it. That last point – in my view – is reasonable; not necessarily because the Empire didn't need apologising for – that is a complex question in itself – but simply because it is irrational to hold *future* generations responsible for policies whose only connection with them is that they were pursued by people who happened to live on the same patch of land, in very different historical circumstances.

By exactly the same token, however, 'pride' in past events – like the British Empire – is equally inappropriate. There are two possible reasons why Blair and Brown latched on to it. The first was to give the Labour Party a mantle of 'patriotism': a quality that was supposed to have electoral appeal, and which it was commonly perceived to have lacked in the past. (Not only Labour; nineteenth-century Liberals had suffered from this too, ever since Disraeli had hijacked patriotism for the Tories in the 1860s and '70s.) Connected with this may have been the need widely perceived at this time in government circles for a more positive image of British (or English) 'national identity' than was thought to be prevalent then. It is well known that Britain is one of the least 'patriotic' countries in the world; that was held to be a weakness. Hence this controversial line in a Home Office 'citizenship' booklet issued in December 2004: 'For many indigenous peoples in Africa and elsewhere the British Empire often brought more regular, acceptable and impartial systems of law and order than many had experienced under their own rulers.' (Controversial it may have been; but the 'often' and 'many' there make it defensible, at least.) The second broad reason for this 'pride' may have been that Blair and Brown were genuinely persuaded by the new view of the Empire, which, as we have seen, had quite a lot going for it: certainly by the side of the crudely reductionist 'anti' one. They were, after all, of the post-imperial generation: exactly the one that was, as suggested earlier, likely to be amenable to this 'reimagining' of the old devil. (Blair and Brown were 44 and 46 years old respectively in 1997.) But whatever the reasons, these views of theirs could be seen to qualify them as 'imperialists', of a kind. They certainly did, all too predictably, in the eyes of their critics.

All this was pretty harmless in itself, except perhaps for those who still had bruises to show (or imagined they had) from the colonial encounter. Even they should not have felt too hurt. The implications of an admiration for the historical Empire will vary according to the political inclinations of those doing the admiring; in right-wingers it is likely to be associated with, say, racism and arrogance, but with a Labour man or woman there is far less danger of that. While the Empire was still a going concern, Labour's record on colonial race relations had usually (not always) been a fairly good one, including in those brief periods when it actually ran it. Blair and Brown clearly associated the Empire, rather selectively, with the spread of law, peace and racial equality: the spin that had been put on it first of all by the interwar Commonwealthists, and then by its more recent apologists. Imperial nostalgia from this quarter was a different thing entirely from a similar *sounding* nostalgia from, say, the overtly racist British National Party. It celebrated the best side of empire, not the worst. By the same token, it was only likely to give rise to well-intentioned policies towards ex-colonies and other 'victim' nations: especially those designed to protect or save their peoples from poverty, starvation, ignorance and disease, rather than more 'strategic', selfish or mercenary ones (though the two sorts could get mixed up).

The new Labour government's early policies in this field – before 9/11 – were mostly of this 'humanitarian' kind. Its trebling of Britain's foreign aid budget, from £1.4 billions in 1997 to a projected £4 billion in 2005, is an example. This was mainly the doing of Clare Short, the dedicated and energetic new Minister for International Development, but it also had Blair's keen support. His more dramatic (because military) interventions in Kosovo (1999) and Sierra Leone (2000) – the former with America, the latter alone – can also be seen in this light. They were to save lives. Neither crisis affected Britain's security, or her material interests to any great extent. Ideology came into it: Blair's support for the government of Ahmad Tejan Kabbah in Sierra Leone, for example, was partly on the grounds that he considered him a good 'modernising' liberal; but it was a less hard-nosed (or 'libertarian') kind of ideology than America's a little later on. Blair's prime motivation appears to have been mainly altruistic, moral, even religious; the sort of thing even religious American Republicans tended to sneer at then. John Kampfner also sees elements of 'imperialism' in it: 'Britain's colonial burden returning', he calls Sierra Leone. But if so, then it was imperialism in the warm, benevolent, rose-tinted – and, it has to be said, largely mythical – sense.

Blair, however, went much further than this, and in ways that can be seen to have been affected far more obviously by Britain's imperial past. This is because he alluded to it, as a reason for assuming the world role he did, even before 9/11 and all that business with the Americans. In November 1997 for example he asserted that 'By virtue of our geography, our history' – that could only mean their imperial history – 'and the strengths of our people, Britain is a global player.' The key statement, however, came a little later, in January 2002, at a 'Partnership Summit' in Bangalore. 'The days of Empire are gone,' he said there: that was of course obligatory. Britain was demonstrably 'not a superpower today'; but she could still take a leading – in this speech he called it a 'pivotal' – role in international affairs.

> In part, this is by virtue of our history. Our past gives us huge, perhaps unparalleled connections with many different regions of the world. We are strong allies of the US. We are part of the European Union. Our ties with the Commonwealth, with India and other parts of this sub-continent, are visibly strengthening. . . .

Much of this, of course, was the legacy of empire, especially those 'huge, unparalleled connections', which Blair obviously thought was still bankable. His Labour predecessor Harold Wilson had had much the same idea. Britain's past, however you regarded it, had left her with a fund of experience and of worldwide relationships that could be utilised, and which placed her in a privileged situation, still, *vis-à-vis* other countries. She could be compared to an ageing roué who, though he may not be able to perform as he once did, retains his memories, and his address book. Lastly, Blair might have got some of his sense of *mission* from the Empire; or rather, from the grand idealistic designs that had undoubtedly once accrued to it, though they had never been at its root. For Blair was determined to spend Britain's inherited capital ambitiously, and for the benefit, as he saw it, of the world.

This is not the place to speculate on the personal origins of his ambition, or hubris, as many characterised it at the time. (Of course it wouldn't be hubris if it worked.) Most biographers comment on the 'lightness' of Blair's ideological baggage when he became Labour leader, his apparent lack of interest in foreign policy before he entered Downing Street, and the mainly 'moral' grounding of his views on the world thereafter; none of which however prevented his developing clear and strong views about it, which were the source of most of his troubles thereafter, as well as of his successes. He is often painted as naïve, but usually on the say-so of the superior, worldly, overcautious Foreign Office types he tended to distrust. 'The cynics say, "Why should we succeed now when we have failed before?"' he once said. 'But that is what they have said throughout human history. If we listened to them we would still be in the Dark Ages.' He certainly rated 'conviction' high, like Margaret Thatcher, whom he admired. He insisted on being trusted, his hackles rising when his honesty was impugned – when the Tory leader called him a 'liar' during the 2005 election campaign, for example – but sometimes gave the impression that he thought this was enough. 'You may disagree with my judgement, but you must accept my integrity,' he said often; which may be little comfort to most people if the judgement is disastrous. He seems to have had an instinctive, ethics-based view of many issues, rather than a deep or a subtle one. 'There is right and wrong. There is good and bad. We all know this, of course, but it has become fashionable to be uncomfortable about such language.' Obviously his religious faith (Christian, veering to Catholic) came in here. He was convinced of his own powers of persuasion, which were in truth remarkable, if not always very long-lasting. On foreign policy issues in particular his broader views, which didn't really surface until a couple of years into his premiership, appear to have been forged in the fires of the two military conflicts he was involved in early on: in Iraq in 1998 (Operation Desert Fox) and Kosovo in 1999. That is a fairly narrow basis for an entire foreign policy 'doctrine'. But this may be doing him an injustice.

That doctrine, in its original version – before, that is, its trajectory became distorted by coming too close to America's sun – was fairly simple, albeit radical. It was not overtly 'imperialist'; indeed, Blair conceived of it as essentially 'internationalist', which is usually taken to be imperialism's antithesis, though we have seen in Britain's case after around 1900 that the two can become conflated. At its core was what Blair called, in his first-ever major foreign policy speech, delivered to the Chicago Economic Club in April 1999, the principle of 'international community'. By that he meant that people all over the world now shared a *common* community, breaking down the old national boundaries between them – the result, of course, of 'globalisation'. So everyone was responsible for everyone else internationally, just as they were – he, as a social democrat, would maintain – at more local levels: a city or a neighbourhood, for example. One implication of this was that national sovereignty should no longer be regarded as so sacrosanct as it used to be; in international law, for example, where almost the only valid ground for war was currently taken to be to counter one nation's aggression against another. In his brief period of immersion in foreign affairs, Blair had seen the blatant shortcomings of that in Africa, the Balkans and Iraq, where before his time the international community had seemed powerless to prevent mass starvation as the result of civil wars, 'ethnic cleansing', or even a potential threat (from 'WMDs') to itself. They needed to widen the rules of engagement, therefore, to enable military intervention by other states in circumstances like these. That was the radical part. On the other hand, such interventions would still need to be sanctioned by the United Nations (once it had rewritten its rules and procedures to take account of this). Blair was quite clear about this. He had even drafted five criteria for intervention, which included – these are singled out because they became significant later on – 'are we sure of our case', 'have we exhausted all diplomatic options', and 'are we prepared for the long term'? So there were rules to be followed.

There was however one other thing. Blair was convinced that it was vital for the United States to be involved in this. She was the most powerful nation in the world; it would not work without her. So the peroration of Blair's Chicago speech was devoted to counselling America against yet another of her periodic retreats into 'isolationism', which he feared was a likelihood, in view of all the flak that President Clinton was currently getting for his 'humanitarian interventions' abroad, especially from Republicans (as we have seen), who might after all be forming the next administration. The way he tried to sell the message to the Americans was by flattering them about their 'values', which he claimed Britain shared; and arguing that the *spread* of those values in the world was vital to their own national interest. 'In the end values and interests merge. If we can establish and spread the values of liberty, the rule of law, human rights and an open society then it is in our national interests too. The spread of our values makes us safer.' That could be said to be the *potentially* imperialist part of the 'Blair doctrine'. That is certainly how it turned out; but only after the American Republican Right had taken it up, with certain changes of its own.

Blair and Bush

The reason this chapter has now come to focus so narrowly on Tony Blair is that he appears to have been responsible for Britain's post-9/11 foreign policy virtually single-handedly. (This is John Kampfner's conclusion, in his *Blair's Wars*, 2003.) Neither of Blair's first two Foreign Secretaries, Robin Cook and Jack Straw, had much of a hand in it. Cook also proclaimed an 'ethical foreign policy', but with a rather different slant: his main ethical priorities were encouraging human rights, and curbing arms sales. He didn't share Blair's vision, and was removed from the Foreign Office in June 2001. When the ill-prepared Straw took over, Blair's course had already been set. He was probably more powerful *vis-à-vis* his Cabinet than any previous British prime minister, though this had been a trend ('presidentialism') that had been developing for years. The Cabinet could have over-ruled him over the Iraq War, of course, and didn't; but several of its members are known to have been privately unhappy (two resigned, Cook and Short), and it is difficult to imagine any of them taking Britain to war in quite the same wholehearted way, or even at all, if he or she had been prime minister in 2001 or 2003. (Nor, probably, people said, would Harold Wilson if he had still been around, in view of his refusal to help President Johnson in quite similar circumstances over Vietnam.) Blair was lucky in Parliament in that although more than half the 'non-payroll' Labour MPs voted against the Iraq War, he still had the Conservative opposition to back him. Most of the general population opposed him. (An anti-war demonstration in London on 15 February 2003 was the largest in British history.) So it was mainly Blair's doing, even though this obviously doesn't exonerate from responsibility those who failed to put a stop to him. This is a chastening thought for historians (like myself) who don't like to attribute 'great' events to single actors, or chance factors. Over on the other side of the Atlantic, of course, you had a similar thing: this time a small group of ideologues surrounding a vacuous president, largely determining – because of another 'chance' (9/11) – the fate of the world. That is equally unsettling.

The course of Blair's foreign policy after 9/11 is well known. He was enormously sympathetic towards and supportive of America in the immediate wake of the atrocity itself; but then wasn't almost everyone in the world? It has become a cliché to say that there probably hasn't been a moment in recent history when America was more widely identified with, even loved; giving the lie to the notion, common in some circles, that 'anti-Americanism' was visceral, unreasoning and indiscriminate. Another common cliché is that this furnished a great opportunity for a new kind of international cooperation, of the kind, perhaps, that Blair had talked about in Chicago, rising from the smoldering ruins of the Twin Towers; but that Bush (and his ideologues) then blew it. They almost seemed to court hostility from their new friends: bullying them, insulting them (literally), refusing to cooperate over what were considered vital issues like global warming, nuclear proliferation and an International Criminal Court (they demanded Americans be immune from it); and making it clear that they would go their own way, regardless of what anyone else thought, in their response to the Al-Qaeda attacks. Was this deliberate? Did the Americans in some perverse way *need* anti-Americanism, perhaps? Or to believe that they were the *only* 'City on a Hill'? Or was it just Bush's rough, Texan way? Whatever it was, it alienated people (especially Labour supporters) in Britain, as well as everywhere else.

The most controversial issue, of course, was the invasion of Iraq in March 2003, highly precipitously, it was generally believed, and possibly illegally – without, that is, a specific mandate from the UN. That contradicted two of Tony Blair's essential 'criteria' for intervention in this kind of situation: 'are we sure of our case?' and 'have we exhausted all the diplomatic options?' A third was contravened when it became clear that no, the Americans *weren't* 'prepared for the long term' in Iraq. Despite this, Blair was one of only a very small number of national leaders who backed the US unquestioningly, and the only one who delivered a significant number of troops. It caused him enormous trouble at home (though not as much as was caused to the Spanish conservative Prime Minister, who was turfed out because of *his* support for the war). Blair said it was because he genuinely believed in the cause (or causes: first disarmament, then regime-change); and because he thought he could best influence President Bush if he kept on the right side of him. Most observers saw very little sign of such influence working, however, apart from Bush's agreement to Blair's failed attempt to get a new prewar UN resolution in March 2003. Blair was hoping for progress over Israel/Palestine – the heart of the Middle East problem, as he (and many others) saw it. He didn't get far with that. On a more mundane – even sordid – level, British companies were given only scraps from the Americans' table when lucrative postwar reconstruction contracts were handed out. The most Blair got out of it all were some standing ovations in Congress. (They loved him.) If Britain was hoping to be an active and contributory part of the new American 'imperialism' therefore – Robin to the US empire's Batman – it didn't quite work out. There were always tensions, especially between Blair's entourage – Jack Straw, for example – and what the latter's opposite number in Washington, Colin Powell, is reputed to have referred to over the phone to him once as the 'fucking crazies' there: the Neocons. (So there were tensions in Washington too.)

Imperialisms compared

The Anglo-American tensions were not over 'imperialism' specifically, of course; but they do highlight the differences between the two countries' imperial styles. Not completely, because Blair himself was not the best conceivable representative of what might be considered the British tradition: his embrace of economic liberalism and 'globalisation' distanced him from old British paternalism, for example; his religious conviction was very different from the solid realism that had governed most British colonial policy in the old days; and both these things, plus his talk of the 'spread of freedom', put him closer ideologically to the Americans, which is one of the reasons he got on so comparatively well with them. (At one point he is supposed to have said that he didn't understand what all the fuss about the 'Neocons' was about.) Neither side made explicit comparisons between their forms of 'imperialism', naturally, because neither wanted to accept that description of what it was doing; and for those who were prepared to acknowledge it, the comparisons were often fairly crude. Usually it just came down to how alike – stained by the sin, or otherwise, of imperialism – they were. The unlikenesses, however, are equally significant. There were several, but they can be grouped into three broad categories. All gave rise to frictions of one kind or another between the Americans and the British in Iraq.

The first had to do with the Americans' overriding emphasis on military force as the main tool of their 'imperialism', by contrast with Britain's more 'persuasive' approach. In part, of course, this derived from the disparity in military strength between the two countries: a disparity which, as we have seen, related not only to their *present* situations, but distinguished America in the early 2000s from Britain at her imperial zenith too. One result of this was to give America more confidence in her armed forces than Britain could ever have (especially, it has to be said, those high-up politicians, like Defense Secretary Rumsfeld, with no military experience – Colin Powell, a distinguished ex-General, was more cautious over this); which is what had inclined Britain more towards diplomatic solutions to international problems – including 'appeasement' – in the past. 'Appeasement' is a word worth mentioning in this context, because it was not only widely deployed at this time to vilify policies that were supposed to be analogous with those of 1930s' Europe (however tenuously), but also – one often gets the impression – thought to tarnish any kind of diplomacy at all. There is also a cultural component to this, as we have seen; especially America's long tradition of colonialist and 'macho' fiction, and, towering over this, the image of the typical 'John Wayne' figure, sorting out problems that the weaker and womanly characters in the film have failed to address – 'honestly', from the barrel of a gun. Many Americans appeared to feel that *not* using force was a sign of weakness. Military violence featured in British imperialism too, of course, including atrocities – massacres, innocent casualties, brutal punishments, torture, etc. – that are fully comparable with what was seen in and surrounding the Afghan and Iraqi wars; but it did not become so much a part of British culture, and, more to the point, it was never seen as a *first* resort in the solution of major international problems, so much as in America's case. It is indisputable now that the Bush (II) administration *wanted* to go to war with Iraq right from the beginning. Its subsequent diplomacy was mainly directed to securing the conditions in which that could be justified: making sure, for example, that the efforts of the weapons inspectors were *seen* to fail (though we now know that they didn't). Blair appears – this is what he always tried to persuade the British people, at any rate – to have still believed and hoped, quite late in the process, that diplomacy could achieve their ends without war. Later on the American administration was clearly highly sceptical of European efforts to *persuade* Iran to come clean about her nuclear capability without being bombed into it. (Unfortunately for the US – fortunately, of course, for Iran – the former seemed too tied up in Iraq to risk another military conflict just then.) That marked a significant difference of imperial 'style'.

It also explains the divergences between them on the question of 'internationalism', which the British, even in their 'high imperial' phase, had never ever disparaged in quite the way that the American 'Neocons' did: John Bolton, for example, Bush's extraordinary choice as US Ambassador to the United Nations in 2005. ('There is no such thing as the United Nations.') Of course, in the high imperial age there was less internationalism around to disparage, though there was some – agreements on this and that. When influential internationalist philosophies arose around the turn of the twentieth century, however – that is, ideas of subsuming national sovereignties in, or subordinating them to, a 'higher' body that would keep the peace between them – Britain was officially broadly sympathetic to them, and she played an active role in the League of Nations (unlike America) when it was set up after the First World War. In her case this was generally regarded as fully consistent with her national interests and traditions, and even with her *imperialism*, as we described its rhetorical transformation in Chapter 1 (the Commonwealth as a kind of proto-League).

Blair's embrace of internationalism in his Chicago speech, therefore, and his concern for the international *legality* of the Iraq War afterwards, were part of a long British tradition which the Empire had scarcely dented, because the latter had not usually been seen as under threat from it. It was different with twenty-first century American 'imperialism'. The reasons for this are complex. The prominence of the Neocons in American government is obviously one. (Britain had her 'crazies' too, but they never came to power, except possibly at one moment – the middle of the First World War and just after – when they were constrained by events.) Their certainty about America's monopoly of wisdom – the 'City on a Hill' and all that – may be another: why consult others when you know you're right? The lower place given to peace on their list of national proprieties is a third: the League of Nations and the United Nations were mainly designed to stop wars, but America didn't necessarily want to do that. A final factor may have been simply America's perceived strength. You don't need to cooperate with others if you have 'full spectrum dominance'. But for whatever reasons, this marks a further difference. British imperialism was 'internationalist' in a way that modern American 'imperialism' is clearly not.

The second category of differences between them relates to their best ideals. Leaving aside for the moment the question of the place of these ideals in the broader scheme of things – by the side of profit, for example, or glory, or domination, or other darker motives for empire – there are clear distinctions that can be drawn between what America and Britain wanted to do for the world (or said they wanted to do for it) in a 'good' way. The best way of characterising these is as 'libertarian' on the one side, and 'humanitarian' on the other. Americans wanted to bring economic and political freedom to peoples. Because of the way 'freedom' was conceived in America, as – chiefly – an absence of restraint, that meant mainly simply *removing* the restraints that currently bound people, especially those imposed by political tyrants, in order to allow freedom to grow. We saw that British Liberals had had much the same idea about 'freedom' in the mid-nineteenth century, but grew sceptical of it later on. British self-styled *imperialists*, who were not usually liberals, looked at 'freedom' in subtly different ways. Democracy, of course, was almost never part of it. It was not part of the main agenda in Britain itself, either, for most of the nineteenth century; during the whole of which Britons nonetheless prided themselves on being 'free'. It is these sorts of 'freedom' that they offered their colonial subjects too (how far they delivered them is another matter); they included security, peace, equal justice, education, health, adequate food, shelter, and protection against exploitation; none of which is incompatible with democracy, of course, but all of which can be seen as distinct. Americans clearly rated these lower than the British. Hence her generally poor record on 'human rights' (Guantanamo Bay, slogan 'Honor Bound to Defend Freedom': were those responsible for that aware of how it would inevitably recall the notorious 'Arbeit macht frei' sign at Auschwitz?); her very enthusiasm for war (how 'free' are you if you are dead?); her Republicans' scorn for the well-meaning 'humanitarian interventions' of Clinton, which we have already mentioned (Chapter 3); and her neglect of Africa, where the issues were mainly humanitarian – because, as Andrew Bacevich puts it, 'Africa doesn't pay'. (Nor, it could be added, does she pose an obvious threat to the US.) Hence Bush's embarrassing brush-offs of Blair over the latter's close-to-the-heart issues of African aid and debt relief in 2004–5. What all this seems to indicate is a markedly different set of liberal-'imperial' priorities between the two allies. For most Americans these were security and the spread of economic and political liberty. For Britons, they also included feeding the hungry, treating the sick, and so on, in a positive, pro-active way: not, that is, relying on 'economic freedom' alone.

This links with the third major area of difference between the two 'imperialisms', which was over the question of 'reconstruction'. Again, two terms can be used as a shorthand to characterise the two approaches: 'regime change', representing the American approach; and 'nation-building', which was much more a British thing. It can also be said to be a more *imperialist* thing, as 'building' a nation implies a more continuous occupation of it than does merely changing its government. That of course was one of the reasons why the Americans didn't want it. They also assumed it wouldn't be necessary. After their ecstatic welcome in the streets – all those flowers and candies – the American liberators would stay just a little while longer to set up an interim administration (probably under a trusted exile), and arrange free and fair elections to legitimise it, after which they could leave. No problem. (Donald Rumsfeld – who appears to have been the main *naïf* here – pencilled in thirty days for this. Then, he thought, they could move on to the next 'rogue state'.) Before and during the Iraq War Tony Blair several times tried to get Bush thinking about postwar planning – 'what happens on the morning after' – 'but found it hard to get him to focus', says Kampfner. This may have been one of the reasons. Their ideology told them that 'planning' wouldn't be necessary. So America ran no risk of becoming enmired, imperially.

The British imperial tradition, of course, was far more pragmatic, and so might have coped better with the ensuing situation – which turned out nothing like Rumsfeld had predicted. For a few years now a handful of people had been arguing that in order to 'rescue' what had come to be dubbed 'failed states', someone – another country, 'powerful, respected and benevolent', in the words of the *Financial Times*'s Martin Wolf in 2001 – would need to go in from the outside and *rule* them. On the other side of the Atlantic Max Boot had exactly the same idea, and actually took the old British Empire as his model; hence the reference to 'self-confident Englishmen in jodhpurs and pith helmets' quoted earlier. Perhaps it could be done 'internationally' rather than by a single 'imperial' power, they both suggested: Boot cited the League of Nations mandates regime as a precedent. The important thing, however, was that the process of nation-building had to be done under supervision, and over time. This was Niall Ferguson's argument too, in his *Colossus: The Rise and Fall of the American Empire* (2004). 'I am all in favour of a ['thirty'] timetable,' he wrote later, 'provided the measurement is years, not days.' But of course that really *would* lead the US into 'imperialism' (which is what Ferguson was openly advocating). Which would in its turn – it has been argued here – necessitate a social transformation in the US itself. That is hard to envisage.

Nonetheless, the contrast between the two approaches is plain. At bottom it could be characterised as one between ideals (American) and experience (British); or ide*ology* and pragmatism; or naïveté and worldly wisdom; or conviction and scepticism; or between the two nations' own very different domestic historical traditions, 'creationist' and 'evolutionary' (see Chapter 3); or (lastly) between simple principle, and lack of it. American 'imperialism' (the theory) worked in a principled way, to transform peoples all at once through revolution; the British sort had always – at least since 1858 – sought to work more slowly and empathetically, with what it found to work with on the ground. There were problems with both ways. With America's, it was that she *only* had the means to effect revolutions, and nothing to pick up the pieces if those revolutions did not turn out right. Soldiers may be good at changing regimes, but are not the best people to rule those regimes sensitively, even if they are not as particularly insensitive as the American ones in Iraq, for example, often revealed themselves – in numerous acts of panic, overreaction, stupidity and cruelty – to be. With the British approach, if it had ever been tried, there were the dangers of patronisation, lack of imagination, conservatism and stagnation; so that the new nations, in the end, would *never* get built. The choice was between John Wayne and Charles Dance (in *The Jewel in the Crown*: one of those nostalgic Indian TV drama serials), neither of them really likely to bring 'failed states' to nationhood, except by provoking the natives against them: which is how most post-colonial states in history have been formed.

In the end the British brand of imperialism appears to have had little or no impact on the American. This is unsurprising; imperialisms don't usually impact on other imperialisms in this kind of way. America's foreign policy in the early 2000s arose from her own material situation, and was determined in its character by her culture. As well as that, there was the fact that America was a mighty superpower, and Britain was just ordinary. What you got in Iraq, therefore, was America doing her own thing mainly, with Britain simply supporting her, on the former's terms. This is not to say that there were not aspects of those terms that Blair did not, independently, go along with. We saw this in his 1999 Chicago speech, some of which actually anticipated parts of the later 'Bush doctrine'. If he was America's 'poodle', therefore, as he was often portrayed, he didn't necessarily need a lead to keep him in line with his master. Nonetheless, the walkies was not always a happy one for him. Bush took him along several paths he would rather not have taken, and barred him from sniffing out some scents of his own. This was 'imperialism' the American way, not the British.

This is why it is sometimes difficult to spot the differences. Most of them were hypothetical. If Britain had had her way more she would have given diplomacy longer to work at the beginning of the crisis; involved the UN more centrally, especially in reconstruction; almost certainly not been so blatantly profiteering (those contracts); been less ideologically driven, or naïve; tried to address the roots of terrorism more (not just the 'evil'); empathised more with cultural differences; settled down for a long postwar occupation – and possibly not got anything done. She would also have liked America to be softer, more 'humanitarian'; shown more concern for poverty, for example, in places like Africa that didn't seem to affect US national interests so directly. That is, if Britain's imperial history, or the 'best' side of it, was anything to go by. That history also seemed to teach her that the alternative American approach was *not* the way to go about things. But then, as Blair said, if they had always listened to history, they would 'still be in the Dark Ages'. Britain's method had been given its chance, and it hadn't succeeded – at least (*pace* Ferguson) on balance. *This* American approach had not really been tried before. It might just work.

Conclusion

Superempire

Modern American 'imperialism' is not like old British imperialism. It is much, much bigger. Britain once had an empire. America now has a superempire. The prefix 'super' is apt because of the slight ambivalence that attaches to it. 'Superman' is either a terrific man, or he is more than a man. Likewise with present-day America. If she isn't a terrific empire – and throughout this book I've consistently refused to pronounce on this, because I don't think it matters, essentially – she is *more* than one. She exceeds any previous empires the world has ever seen: for example in the spread of her cultural and economic influence ('imperial' or not); in her military dominance; and in the extent of her ambition – or that of her leading 'imperialists' (or their super-equivalents) – to remodel the world in her own image. If that still does not qualify her as an empire, then it is because she has no desire to do this 'formally'. But then neither did Britain, for much of the time she is generally acknowledged to have been most 'imperialistic', in the nineteenth century. Leaving that aside, however: America's reluctance to take on all the traditional trappings of empire doesn't necessarily make her *less* than one. She is transcending the category. Nothing quite like this has ever been seen before.

There are many similarities between the two 'empires'. Both countries' *denials* of their 'imperialisms', or at least of their imperialistic intents, are one. Capitalism is a second. Both 'empires' have arisen and then spread around the world on the crests of waves of expanding commerce and foreign investment, called 'free trade' in the one case, 'globalisation' in the other. Oil is a common factor later on. Good intentions are another. Both the British and the Americans claimed to be 'civilising' forces, even 'liberating' ones. Both 'empires' have imperial *precedents*: Britain's stretching back to the sixteenth century, America's to her national origins, at least. This is despite the latter's frequent protestations of virginity in this regard, which are obvious nonsense. There is a particularly strong link between Britain's 'informal imperialism' of the mid-nineteenth century, associated ideologically with Richard Cobden, and American expansionary commercial policy and philosophy in the twentieth. Many of the nitty-gritty details of the two countries' 'imperial' histories are uncannily alike, especially with regard to the colonisations of, for example, Australia and the American West. These include the 'atrocities'. Some of the sites of modern American 'imperialism' were British imperial stamping-grounds earlier, notably Afghanistan and Iraq. Both 'imperialisms' related to their *domestic* societies in similar ways; though it has been argued here that America's colonial experience scarred her culture more. Even their 'anti-imperialisms' took very similar forms. All this accounts for the parallels that are often drawn between nineteenth-century British imperialism and modern American 'imperialism', and the 'lessons' that are supposed to follow from these.

The differences, however, are more significant. The major one is the ideological component of the American variety, which, whatever its true place in the overall picture – whether it is a genuine *reason* for American foreign policy, or just a cynical cover for more sordid motives – is what makes American 'imperialism' appear most distinct from the British. In this respect, other imperialisms may be a closer fit. The two most obvious ones are the Napoleonic Empire of the turn of the nineteenth century, and the Soviet one of the twentieth; both of which had global aspirations, like the Americans, and were fired by ideological certainties that enabled their conquests to be presented as 'liberations', though their victims might disagree. (There have also been religious movements, especially Christian and Muslim, that shared these characteristics.) The British Empire had elements of this, but in a much weaker form. No British imperialist (except a few 'crazies' at the margins) ever thought that the British, or British values, might come to rule the world. They never even came close to this in practice. For a start, Britain always had powerful military rivals, in a way that America no longer has. So, for that matter, did revolutionary France and the USSR. Britain also never had quite the cultural self-confidence of these other imperialists: the belief that she had found the Way and the Light for all humanity, and that consequently the rest of humanity – those still wandering blindly – must be initiated into them. You can see something of this early on, perhaps, in the zeal of some of those who legislated for India (especially from London) before the shock of the 'Mutiny'; and in the quiet confidence of the 'Cobdenites', who believed that 'free trade' would eventually make everything right for everyone. Many nineteenth-century Britons thought they were 'ahead' of most of the rest of the world in their economic and political development ('freedom'), and consequently that others were bound to follow them; but none – that I have discovered – believed that they were there, in sight of the 'end of history', *yet*. So far as the men who actually *ruled* Britain's empire were concerned, there was even less of this. For reasons that have been explained, mainly social, they tended to be pragmatists, and even 'relativists', rather than ideologues. Their basic rationale for what they were doing was not that they were necessarily morally better than the people they were ruling, or brighter, or more enlightened, particularly; but simply that they were better than them *at* ruling. One reason for this was that they *tolerated* their subjects' cultures and customs in a way that ideologues – contemporary ideologues, at any rate – were unlikely to; which accounts for their success – success, that is, at managing to hold on to rule their subjects for so long; but also, on the other side, for their failures, by and large, when it came to 'remodelling' them. Britain's was not an ideologically driven empire, in the same way that the modern American 'empire' makes itself out to be. That's where the comparison mainly falls down.

The side of history?

This ideological aspect of current American foreign policy is striking. To a certain extent it is *accidental*, the result of a combination of three literally surprising events: George W. Bush's narrow and disputed Presidential electoral victory in November 2000 (a swing of one vote in the US Supreme Court and it could have gone the other way); the consequent elevation to positions of great influence over a weak-minded President of a tiny neoconservative clique that might have remained as marginal as Britain's 'crazies' otherwise; and the attacks of 9/11, which enabled that clique shortly afterwards to set in motion its implicitly imperialistic agenda for the 'new American century'. That seems an incredibly narrow fulcrum for such a significant turn of events. *One judge!* And the world so changed! When future historians come to analyse the causes of the American superimperialism of the early twenty-first century, they are going to be hard pressed to weave a 'general theory', like the ones that are supposed to account for the European imperialisms of the later nineteenth century, out of that. Again: this is not a comfortable thought for those historians – like me – who don't like to think of great events hinging on 'accidents'.

On the other hand, however, we can't really be sure of how Bush's Democratic rival Al Gore might have reacted to 9/11; or of what a Bush presidency starting in 2005 – brought to power by the perceived pusillanimity of Gore's first term, perhaps – would have done. Perhaps it would have worked out much the same in the end. There are certain underlying trends in history that these surprising happenings *don't* seem to buck: the development and spread of capitalism in the world, for one, with which the particular kind of 'freedom' America is seeking to impose on the world – *markets* and democracy – is perfectly consistent. Old Marxists should have no problem with these things. Marx and Lenin predicted that capitalism would grow more desperate, illiberal and imperialist in the future; recent international events could certainly be read in this way. Then, thought Marx and Lenin, it would collapse under the force of the internal contradictions thus revealed. Well, we'll see. For a time it used to be thought that Marx's predictions had been invalidated by, firstly, Russia's premature revolution – that didn't follow Marx's plan at all; then by the success of halfway-house social democracies in Europe, which also weren't foreseen; and lastly, by the collapse of the first Marxist state, which was misread as bringing down Marx*ism* too. In fact that last event could be said to have returned the Marxist train to its old theoretical tracks. Capitalism is just now exhibiting the signs of desperation the old Marxists predicted for it, when it needs to conquer the world in order to survive. (Take oil.) No one could have foreseen that it would happen in quite this extraordinary way, with Osama bin Laden's help, and all the rest; but, still, it fits. We still don't know whether the rest of the Marxist-Leninist prediction will come to pass: contradiction, collapse, a proper revolution; but there are some promisingly ominous clouds on the horizon, and it is still early days yet. This isn't necessarily my reading of these events, by the way (certainly not the predictive part); but it is certainly a plausible one. There are also some other general theories that could be said to fit. Samuel Huntington's 'clash of civilizations' (modernity versus Islam, roughly) is one. The premillennial dispensationalist thing is obviously a third. There may be others. We don't need, if we don't want, to surrender entirely to chance.

Further: it is possible to descry many of the key elements of this sudden present-day American superimperialism in the much broader culture of the nation, going back many years. We have alluded to this: America's strongly imperialist tradition (by most definitions) for a start; but further than that – and much more important – some of her extraordinary national myths, such as the belief that she has been uniquely *innocent* of imperialism, and indeed superior to all countries in the history of the world in almost every other essential regard – in other words, her 'exceptionalism'. This must be why when Neocons claim that American business, domination, conquest or whatever must be good for everyone in the world, it is so widely accepted at home. The idea has usually been around in American political and religious culture in one guise or another, as we noted at several points in the 'historical' section of this book (Chapter 2). It may have been an accident that released it; but it was always there to be released.

The other way for generalists to cope with all this would be if this phase turned out to be only temporary. Even the grandest theories of history can accommodate the occasional blip. The American superempire is bound to collapse, and soon. Then America can return to a more 'normal' line of policy, 'imperialist' or otherwise; and historians can trust again to their broad, non-accidental, trends. There are a number of people predicting this – just as they did, incidentally, at Britain's supposed imperial zenith, around 1900. (In fact the British Empire was already on the slide then.) There were two main factors behind that latter prediction. One was very general indeed: the example of all previous empires in history, but especially the Roman (which was the British imperialists' favourite), all of which, without exception, had ultimately succumbed to the tendency known (following Gibbon, the chronicler of the Roman Empire's last years) as 'decline and fall'. It seemed to be an iron law. The other reason for thinking it could apply to the British Empire then, or very soon after, was that several of its potential nemeses could already be seen hoving into view over the horizon, of which the most likely – the most widely predicted, at any rate – was the United States of America. So this was foretold. A similar process is going on today, with a number of modern Cassandras predicting the decline of the American superempire: through overstretch; financial weakness (the 'deficit'); terrorism; foreign rivalry (China – the warship on America's horizon); moral turpitude (Nye's 'rotting from within'); implosion – the contradiction that lies at the heart of the idea of a 'liberal' state dominating others (the thing that brought the British Empire down – is this the same as the *capitalist* contradiction?); or simply the Iron Law. It could all blow up in America's face.

Against all this are those who argue that the 'exceptional' nature of America's 'empire', and the fact that – *pace* Marx and Lenin – it has 'history' on its side (Condoleezza Rice), will save it in the end. We have seen that most of the exceptions that are often listed for it are not exceptional at all, certainly if you are comparing it with the British Empire, which also claimed many of them but 'declined and fell' nonetheless. In reality, the only truly exceptional feature of the USA is her *belief* in her exceptionalism – the myth, or delusion that she is different in the ways she thinks she is; but that could be enough to keep her 'empire' going on its own. Myths are powerful things. They may be able to overcome even the most iron of historical precedents. Trends can be bucked. Conditions change, making policies that failed in one set of them quite viable in another. A state might just get lucky. Or its policies may not in fact be straight repeats of previous ones, but have important differences, that can *make* all the difference to their outcomes. This is why it is important to be clear about the unique qualities of present-day American superimperialism; which, even if they don't include many of the ones that are widely attributed to it, may possibly be crucial all the same. America may have cracked it. 'In the end,' claims a recent *Patriot's History of the United States* (by Larry Schweikart and Michael Allen, 2005), 'the rest of the world will probably both grimly acknowledge and grudgingly admit that, to paraphrase the song, God has "shed His grace on thee"' – the 'thee' being, of course, America. (The phrase comes from Katherine Lee Bates's 'America the Beautiful'.) That should keep the new superempire going in one form or another for some time; possibly even for ever and ever, Amen. We have noticed the strong religious flavour to this before, right back to Winthrop's 'Citty upon a Hill'. It was probably needed, in order to sustain this enormous leap of faith.

Whether it would sustain the American superempire itself was another question. That really depended on America's having got it right about her 'way', and its intrinsic validity and attraction to other peoples, once they had had their chains cast from them, and could choose how they were governed for themselves. Were American 'values' universal, as we heard Condoleezza Rice claiming in 2000? Many people disputed this. The counter argument, of course, was that they had their origins in and were defined by a particular culture (modern America's), and so were not necessarily applicable to other places and times. This could be said of any system of values. 'Like everything else,' wrote a Sri Lankan commentator in April 1999 (in response to Blair's Chicago speech about 'universal values'), 'human rights . . . are not absolute and are relative. They are relative to the culture. The present day human rights are relative to the present West, which has been successful in establishing their hegemony over the entire world to a large extent.' A slightly less relativistic position on this would be to say that there *are* some basic universal values, but that it is difficult for one country – soaked as it is in its own peculiar culture – to say what these are, and avoid muddying them with its more parochial ones. In America's case it is easy (for outsiders) to see where this has distorted her 'take' on human rights: the stress on 'markets', for example, and the low priority accorded to issues like peace, welfare and feeding the hungry, which seem to matter more to Britain. Whatever the merits of any of these cases may be, they illustrate how tricky the idea of 'universality' is. (This is before we even consider America's *practice* of the values she professes, like democracy, free trade and the rule of law: that 2000 Presidential election, for example; agricultural protectionism; and Guantanamo Bay.) If the 'values' you are being asked to take on board are *not* self-evidently general human ones, then it may be difficult to get them accepted voluntarily. They look like 'imperialist' impositions. And that, of course, provokes resistance. Imperial Britain found this, a hundred times.

In Britain's case one solution was to take over her ungrateful pupils and rule them directly, hoping to convince them of some of *her* values ultimately, but recognising that it might take many decades. This is Niall Ferguson's prescription for countries like Iraq. (In one place he reckons it will take seventy years of foreign rule to establish democracy there.) But that is problematical for America. It was fairly problematical for Britain, which in the nineteenth century was almost as liberal capitalist as America is today, with consequently the same instinctive prejudices against 'government' of all kinds, including imperial; but which also had a small class of people that relished it (and were pretty useless doing anything else), and so could actually take the job on. Even then the human and financial resources she possessed for this purpose were strictly limited, which meant – as we saw – that they couldn't be very effective, especially when it came to 'nation-building'. America's situation is much worse. She doesn't have nearly so much of a governing class or ethos. She has gone too far along the liberal capitalist road, casting both of them behind her. To build or rebuild either, in order to sustain a more 'formal' American empire, would involve radical changes in her social structure and culture which it is almost impossible to conceive. It probably isn't viable.

There is another consideration too. The situation of America as the first 'sole' superpower in the world may give a false impression of what she is able to achieve there militarily. She certainly isn't *all*-powerful. Terrorism, whatever we may think of the morality of it, tends to even up the scales when it comes to relative 'strengths'. That, and more traditional kinds of guerrilla warfare, have tied America down in Afghanistan and Iraq in a way that makes it difficult for her to *extend* her 'imperial' influence to other countries which might (in her view) require it. Everyone assumes (this is written in the summer of 2005) that she has other targets in her sights – Iran, North Korea, Syria; the first two almost certainly more potentially dangerous to her and the world than Iraq ever was – but she can do little about them while she is still preoccupied militarily in these other places. Already her generals are complaining of 'overstretch'. People worry about the 'body bag' factor: the long-term reaction of an American people that is not intrinsically 'imperialist' (any more than the British people were) to the military casualties that long occupations of countries, against fierce resistance, would inevitably entail. There is also the danger of a *liberal* reaction in America against this, like the one over Vietnam. America's military 'hegemony', great as it is, is not absolute. (Her economic and cultural dominance may have been exaggerated, too.) Perhaps she isn't so different from previous empires after all. The Iron Law may apply to her as well.

This is why it is so vital to her that her ideology is sound. If it is, then there will be no need to resort to formal imperialism to achieve her aims. This is how it should work – everyone wants 'democracy'. It is also good for America and the world that everyone gets democracy, because democratic regimes don't fight each other, and don't harbour 'evil' people – 'terrorists' – the way tyrannies do. Not all people realise that they want democracy yet, but they will, because 'history' is moving that way. If America were to wait, then it would – presumably – spread everywhere in time. Unfortunately she can't wait, because of the present threat to her own national security that is posed by those evil terrorists in their tyrannical safe havens, like Afghanistan and – ahem! – Iraq. So she needs to take a hand. Luckily, this need not involve her in too many obligations ultimately, because of that 'history' thing. A quick insertion, a frenzy of physical activity, plant the seed, withdraw, and a democracy will be born. The mother, shocked at first by the violation, will grow to love her new baby quite soon. The nations around her, seeing how happy she is, will all want their little democracies too. Hopefully, these will be achieved more consensually. The Americans can then go back to their homeland, secure with this new community of free, safe peoples around them, and proud of their role in starting it all off. That is, if this works. It may do. If not, they're in a mess.

The British Empire as a model

Rape is a common metaphor for imperialism. It may be an unfair one. The problems with regarding all imperialism in this light are, firstly, that there were many varieties of it, some of them relatively gentle – the historian Geir Lundestad has even identified an 'imperialism by invitation'; and secondly, that this takes no account of the alternatives – what might have become of peoples if they had not been, in any given situation, imperialised. The most likely alternative to British imperialism during most of its history was someone else's, which – as Niall Ferguson rightly points out – could well have been 'worse'. (Britain essentially won India in the eighteenth century from the French, and then defended it against the Russians: that was what she was doing most of the time in Afghanistan. If she had not annexed South Africa, the slave-owning Dutch would have done so. In the twentieth century her main rival in Southeast Asia was Japan.) Even if places like Africa had been left to themselves in a formal sense in the nineteenth century – and this was not out of the question; we have seen that much of what is conventionally called the 'scramble for Africa' consisted in fact of a series of agreements among the European powers to enable them to avoid ruling it – it did not follow that they would not have been tyrannised in other ways: by unscrupulous and unrestrained Western capitalists, for example, or their own bloody despots. (Europe is not the only continent to have suffered from these.) Domestic rape is as common as violation by strangers. Look at Saddam Hussein.

In the nineteenth century imperialism appeared much more morally acceptable than it does today. That's why the Americans did so much of it, almost without noticing. This was partly because 'advanced' nations regarded 'primitive' ones more disparagingly then; partly because the idea of the 'nation' itself was not so firmly fixed then as it became later; and partly because people had this idea that weak nations sometimes needed to be protected by stronger ones, rather than left to the mercy of these predators. This is still a consideration. It is what lay at the root, of course, of Blair's and Clinton's doctrine of 'humanitarian intervention', before that was hijacked by the Bush administration's policy of intervention in the interests of American security; and Blair's call for the rules about 'nationality' – that national integrity is inviolate, and should always be respected except in cases where a nation is attacking another nation – to be reconsidered. The problem of 'rogue' and 'failed' states is as great as it ever was, and more urgent now because of their possible wider repercussions: 9/11, and all that. This is the argument for rehabilitating imperialism today, either unashamedly, or in some kind of semantic disguise. Failed states need successful states to pick them up and revive them. That must be better than leaving them to fester, with all the suffering to themselves and danger to others that festering brings.

This is where the old British Empire is sometimes ushered into the picture, newly dusted down and spruced up, as a model or precedent for the present day. One can see why. It wasn't all bad. It was natural to blame it, perhaps, for everything that was wrong in the world (or at least, in its ex-colonies) immediately after its fall: there's nothing like beating an empire when it's down. One can see traces of this still. Those embarrassed by virulent anti-gay feeling among West Indians, for example, still sometimes hold British imperialism responsible for that. (They'll be blaming George III for homophobia in the American Midwest next.) As well as being patronising towards the West Indians – after all these years, can't they think for themselves? – this also attributes too *much* to the influence of the British Empire: exaggerates its power. Chapter 1 was largely about that. By the same token, of course, the beneficial effects of British imperialism shouldn't be overplayed, either. Still, there were some. There was a lot that was attractive and – I would say – 'good' about many, perhaps most, of the men who actually ran the British Empire in the nineteenth and early twentieth centuries: highly dedicated people, with a devotion to public service that is seen less and less these days; there for the long haul, not just fly-by-nights; benevolent for the most part in their *intentions*, at any rate; protective, especially against capitalist exploitation; and usually tolerant. They did an amazing job for the most part in keeping order and maintaining justice over vast tracts of territory, despite their tiny numbers, and the physical privations they often had to endure. Materially their achievements were considerable. The British were particularly good at this, by comparison with other colonial powers: a fact that is still sometimes acknowledged today. ('You ought to be thankful for being colonized by the British,' writes a

Vietnamese to an Indian in 2005. 'At least you got a railway system to show for your pains. The French colonized us and all we got were brothels and whorehouses.') There were worse fates – much worse – that could befall peoples in the nineteenth and twentieth centuries than being taken in hand by these men. The British Empire had its positive aspects. It is possible that the new American superempire could learn something from it; so long as it chooses the right bits of it to learn from.

This, however, is the difficulty. In the first place, what has just been described is not the only side of the British Empire, because the men who 'ran' it were not the only ones representing it. Even they – high-minded as they generally were – were not entirely dependable; there were many bad eggs among them, and even the better eggs had their bad points. Among these were a stifling conformity; lack of imagination; conservativeness (all carefully instilled in them at their 'public' schools); and a notable lack of skills in the art of 'nation-building'. In addition to these men, and greatly outnumbering them, were all those other sorts of imperialists we listed in Chapter 1, most damagingly, probably, the settlers, soldiers and missionaries, the first two of whom were responsible for most of the atrocities that also need to be brought into the overall colonial picture on the debit side – Amritsar, the Kenya 'Emergency', various exterminations of natives, and so on; and the third of whom, the missionaries, provoked some of the worst problems – the Indian 'Mutiny', for one. Of course these horrors weren't *typical* of the British Empire, but they were *characteristic* of it, and may be so of imperialisms everywhere. (Iraq's present occupiers are already duplicating many old British imperial atrocities.) Not all imperialists are rapists; but imperialism always seems to bring a certain amount of rapine in its train. That is not the kind of lesson we want the Americans to copy today.

The more positive lessons, however, may be beyond them. I have suggested the reason for this already. The days of a more direct and benevolent form of empire are over. They were brought to an end when liberal capitalism finally (presumably) triumphed; or, rather, when the most liberal capitalist society in the world became the single most powerful one. Capitalism is incompatible with imperialism *of this kind.* This may read strangely to those accustomed to thinking that imperialism is a function of capitalism *essentially*, its 'last stage', according to V. I. Lenin's influential analysis of it – that is, a device capitalism resorts to in order to delay its inevitable collapse. This is still a plausible explanation for many of the expansionary features of global capitalism in the late twentieth and early twenty-first centuries, as I have suggested already; but it never did seem to fit British *paternalistic* imperialism very well. That is much more convincingly seen as a throwback to *pre*-capitalist ways of doing things, admixed, as we suggested earlier (Chapter 1), with an element of new *anti*-capitalist social philosophy; neither of which was ever very potent in the USA, and both of which declined even further both there and in most other countries of the world under the impact of 'globalisation'. Britain still retains traces of the former, which is supposed to have made her administration of Basra in the south of Iraq after 2003 more sensitive than the Americans' further north (that at any rate was what her generals said, though by the autumn of 2005 that claim was beginning to wear rather thin); but probably not enough to mount a viable 'paternalistic' operation more widely, even if America were willing to turn her responsibilities over to her. (There are simply not enough Charles Dances.) The dominant ethos of a developed capitalist economy like hers clearly militates against this; which is why the US genuinely doesn't want to 'rule' other peoples, and appears to be not very good at it.

If she doesn't need to – if the world can be 'democratised' relatively easily in the way some of her ideologues appear to believe, and with 'reasonable' people being democratically elected: not anti-American Islamicists, for example – there is, of course, no problem. (What a wonderful day that will be!) History suggests, however – only *suggests*, mind, no more than this – that things don't usually work out this way. Benevolent motives do not always have bene*ficent* outcomes. That is even when they truly are benevolent, wanting nothing but the best for their bene*fici-aries*; and disregarding the dogmatism, the insensitivity and the self-delusion that are often aspects of benevolence, as well as the *less* benevolent motives that inevitably accompany it – the greedy men following in the godly men's tracks. Benevolence from the outside is often resented, perhaps unfairly; Kipling referred to this in his famous lines about incurring 'The blame of those ye better, / The hate of those ye guard', quoted already; and it is also implied in those sour words in Schweikart and Allen's *Patriot's History*, about everyone eventually 'grudgingly' admitting that America was right all along. This is also understandable, however: would any of us relish being told how to behave by anyone who doesn't know us, especially someone who is not behaving particularly well himself in our front yard? People have their dignity. Nations have their dignity too: much more so now than in the nineteenth century, when this factor did not need to be taken into account so much. (Then not every people was thought to merit being counted a 'nation': 'inferior' ones, for example. That is not a respectable position today.)

These, then, are the main arguments against imperialism, of any unilateral kind, 'formal' or 'informal', at the present time. It can be malevolent, or have malevolence mixed in with it; it is usually insensitive, especially administered by people who aren't trained for this kind of thing (and even by many who are); it is bound to be *regarded* as malevolent and insensitive even if it isn't; and it is consequently likely to be counter-productive. It is also simply impossible, in the light of social and economic trends. It *can* give rise to 'free' nations; but usually by provoking rebellion *against* it.

Internationalist imperialism

All this isn't an entirely new situation. Of course some aspects of it are: 9/11 and WMDs, particularly. The more general issues, however – of what to do about 'failed' states or peoples, instability, foreign tyrannies, closed societies, religious fanaticism, even terrorism (on a lesser scale) – all these dogged Britain (and of course other countries) in the nineteenth and early twentieth centuries, as they do all of us today. They are constant problems.

There was a great debate about them a hundred years ago, just like now, and carried on in very similar terms. At the root of it lay this question, the one Tony Blair thought he was formulating in a new way in his Chicago speech (1999): that bearing in mind that there was a great deal of avoidable suffering and also danger in the world, which was *not* attributable to imperialism, was it justifiable to *invoke* imperialism – of one sort or degree or another, from temporary intervention to full-scale rule – to try to put it right? Even turn-of-the-twentieth-century socialists, some of them, believed it was. This is James Ramsay MacDonald – later Britain's first Labour prime minister – in 1901:

> So far as the underlying spirit of Imperialism is a frank acceptance of national duty exercised beyond the nation's political frontiers, so far as it is a claim that a righteous nation is by its nature restless to embark upon crusades of righteousness wherever the world appeals for help, the spirit of Imperialism cannot be condemned. Morality is universal. . . . I want to make it clear that however successful designing men may be in prostituting the high purposes of the nations to their own ends, or however imperfectly the nations themselves interpret their ideals in their political policies, the compulsion to expand and assume world responsibility is worthy at its origin.

'We must not lightly dismiss the claim which every vital people makes,' he wrote on another occasion, 'that it is the chosen instrument for the advancement of good in the world.' On the surface that looks like a clear endorsement of 'liberal imperialism'; an astonishing affirmation – bearing in mind its antiquity – of America's claims today.

But we need to read on. MacDonald was more cautious than this. He was making a theoretical case for imperialism; but the practical flaws in it, he thought, outweighed this. One was the 'empire strikes back' factor. 'The democracy of Britain is beginning to assume more and more the functions and the mental state of the Indian official; of the South-African nigger-driver. . . . The events in Africa of the last year or two [this is in 1898] have brought sentiment in this country nearer and nearer to a lynching potentiality.' Secondly: 'the fact is, civilization is often the *excuse* of imperialism. . . . Empire follows the course of gold reefs [today, read 'oilfields'] rather than the shadows of human degradation.' Thirdly: 'the different civilising value of nations cannot be assessed by any impartial and expert assessor'; in other words, it wasn't necessarily the best 'civilisers' (today, spreaders of 'freedom'), who got the chance to 'civilise', simply the strongest. In today's terms: just because the US is in a *position* to do this, it doesn't necessarily follow that she is the ideal nation to do it. Indeed, the opposite might even be said. And lastly, wrote MacDonald: 'civilized standards' – today, human rights or values – were relative.

> Civilization is not expressed by the reading of the Bible, the drinking of Rum, and the weaving of cotton [we can all think of modern equivalents], for there are other civilizations besides that of the West. When we have developed the sense of ascertaining, as open-minded inquirers, how far civilization differs with climate and other circumstances, and how far its habits must vary with different peoples – how far, for instance,

English civilization can no more be carried to India by
Englishmen and lived up to there by them than they can carry
ice in their luggage – we cannot pretend to be a great civilizing
agency.

He elaborated on this. No civilisation was better than any
other; they were simply different. 'Every civilization has some
political, social or ethical excellence which in that respect may
place it superior to the propagandist's [i.e. the imperialist's]
civilization itself.' And he gave examples. That is interesting in
today's context, because it is an *anti*-imperialist argument, or
set of arguments, that takes on board the problems that
present-day imperialists (Britain) and superimperialists
(America) say they are grappling with, but with a far more
sophisticated understanding than theirs. To me, although
MacDonald was by no means a great or original thinker (or, as
it happens, a very successful prime minister), his musings on
this topic seem way ahead of today's debate.

This is probably due to the fact that MacDonald's generation
had long experience of formal imperialism, albeit from the blunt
end, which Bush's and Blair's don't have. Neither Bush nor Blair is
any kind of a historian, either, so they are unlikely to learn any of
this vicariously. (Some of the Neocons are apparently interested
in history, but mainly ancient Roman – this was Leo Strauss's
speciality – which doesn't teach quite the same things. This is
something else they have in common with nineteenth-century
British imperialists.) For MacDonald and his fellow radical
critics, neither imperialism nor anti-imperialism was the answer
to the problems they *agreed* with the liberal imperialists were
afflicting their world (and in slightly different forms are afflicting
ours): imperialism for the reasons just listed, and which seem
vividly illustrated in the American case today; and anti-*formal*
imperialism – the Cobdenite road, traces of which can also be
seen there – because of the licence that gave to unscrupulous

capitalist companies to 'exploit' the weak. Their solution, worked out as both those alternatives were coming to appear somewhat tarnished, was a kind of middling or 'third' way: essentially an *internationalised form of imperialism*, where the responsibility for 'nation-building' could be dispersed and legitimised, hopefully on the basis of a more consensual understanding of 'universal values' than one country could be expected to have on its own. This finds an echo in the thinking of Tony Blair, before his close association with the very unilateralist Bush singed his internationalist wings. It was tried once, after the First World War, and at the insistence of the USA, of all countries, in the form of the League of Nations' 'mandates' system (later taken over by the UN). It was not a notable success then, partly because of America's refusal to take practical responsibility for her conception; but – as we have suggested in other contexts – one historical failure does not necessarily rule out success a second time around. (Blair was right here, too.)

Progress

That was the 'progressive' solution in 1900. But 'progressive' is liable to change over time. Remember how only twenty or thirty years ago, social democracy used to be regarded as 'progressive' too? Now it appears to be merely a brief diversion in humanity's progress towards the real 'end of history'; an interruption, a step back, a dead end. 'History marches towards markets and democracy'; a market-orientated *type* of democracy, that is, where competition is all, and cooperation, whether in domestic or in international affairs, simply slows things down. Last year's progressives are today's reactionaries. We need to go with the new flow.

If we regard history in this light, then the relationship between the old British imperialism and the new American seems relatively straightforward. The one followed on from the other, but only after the former (the British) had experienced a diversion of its own. The first 'open door empire' was the one the British believed they were building in the middle of the nineteenth century, though they were as reluctant as the later Americans to call it that, because of the negative associations the 'e'-word had accrued to it. It consisted of an expanding free trade *imperium* that was uniquely beneficent, because it didn't oppress anyone; was bound to bring 'freedom' and peace in its train; and, as a result, inevitably spelled the death of 'imperialism' of the more conventional kind.

The problem with this programme *then*, however, was that it became compromised: firstly by the existence, side by side with it, of a number of conventional colonies, inherited from a less enlightened time; secondly, by the survival of a class in British society that didn't share the free traders' views of 'freedom' and the like – their particular *take* on freedom, that is; and thirdly, by what might be seen as some problematical aspects of the project itself – the difficulty of creating the *conditions* for free trade, for example, especially in 'backward' parts of the world, local people's resistance to it, the social disruptions it caused among them (just as the growth of free market capitalism had done in Britain earlier), foreign jealousies (though foreign countries should not have been jealous of what was bound to enrich them as well as Britain), and *possibly* some 'contradictions' intrinsic to it. This led to a kind of metamorphosis of British imperial policy in the later nineteenth century, at least in part, from free trade or 'informal', to annexationist or 'formal'; adding to the stock of British conventional colonies in a way that was totally unforeseen by the original free trade ideologues, and greatly deprecated by their successors; but which seemed *at that time* to be the 'progressive' way. It was around then for example that Lord Rosebery, the leading 'Liberal Imperialist' of the time, dismissed the old ways, picturesquely, as a 'fly-blown phylactery' from a previous age. The future then seemed to lie with the great formal empires: British, French, Russian and American. (At that period, of course, the Americans showed every sign of joining in the game.) Yet again, 'progressive' had shifted. As well as an imperialist, Rosebery was a social reformer: almost a social democrat. (The party he led on the London County Council was called the 'Progressives': named after the exactly contemporary American tendency.) That was the beginning of the age when free marketism, both at home and abroad, at least in its less restrained forms, was coming to be seen as *passé*; before the circle turned again.

British *formal* imperialism eventually – quite soon, in fact – collapsed, because of its intrinsic weaknesses (contradictions?), which came to the surface, as they were bound to, when it became clear that more effort, commitment, men and money would be required to sustain it than in the period when Britain had first accumulated her colonies, both formal and informal, overseas. *Then* she had been able to do it liberally; consistently, that is with her proud traditions of *domestic* liberty (it could be different abroad). After 1900 this became more difficult. Imperial zealots tried to get her to change her domestic spots to cope with this new situation, to little avail. The Empire was able to stagger on a few more years, but only because other nations didn't challenge it, though they were in a position to. When they did, it gave up the ghost. So did other European empires (except the Russian, for a while). This of course was predictable, under the liberal historicist scenario. In America, Sumner Welles proclaimed (or actually anticipated, for this was in 1942) 'the end of the era of imperialism'. In a formal sense, it was.

But not in any other. What essentially happened in the second half of the twentieth century was not the finish of imperialism *per se*, but its return to the form it had first taken in Britain around 1850. It was America, now, that took up the torch that had been dropped by Britain shortly after then. Again, the similarities are striking: including the idealistic claims that were made for it, and the insistence that, as a result, it could not be called imperialism *really*. The differences were, firstly, America's huge dominance; secondly, that some of the values attaching to 'open door imperialism' were significantly different from before, as a result partly of this (America's peculiar culture) and partly of the *hardening* of liberal thought generally in the intervening century; and thirdly, that two of the factors that had compromised the ideal in its original British form were no longer to be found in America – a surviving formal empire (after the Philippines had been got rid of), and an imperial ruling class. Which still, however, left the third compromising factor: the intrinsic difficulties of the project in 'the field'; and left America without Britain's means of coping with those problems, which was to take over the problem countries formally. That probably ensured that the same kind of metamorphosis would not happen to the American empire as had happened to the British. It would not turn 'conventional'. But it didn't dispose of the difficulties, of course.

Whether those difficulties can be dealt with within the framework of the new 'progressive' vision of human development is hard to say. The Americans are placing a great deal of hope – far more than their Victorian predecessors – in, firstly, their grasp of the direction that 'history' is taking; secondly, their military superiority; and thirdly, perhaps, God; but all these may be questionable. History may be more complicated than people like Condoleezza Rice assume. Ways can be found around conventional military hegemony, as we have seen in Iraq. America could still collapse through 'overstretch', or capitalist contradictions. (Or because, as John Winthrop warned, with 'the eies of all people' upon her, God believes she has let Him down.) If internationalism has been ruled out of the equation, then there would seem to be no alternatives beyond *liberal* imperialist success – a world of democracies that won't go to war with each other, with America and Britain proudly basking in the glory; secondly, a perpetual state of *military* imperialism against those who resist the new dispensation; or thirdly, some form of *post*-imperial collapse. Unless, perhaps, the 'progressive' wheel turns once more, towards MacDonaldite *international* imperialism – or Blairite 'international community-ism' – again. Which, if things go badly enough, and 'superimperialism' comes to be seen to be as tarnished as ordinary imperialism was in MacDonald's time, it might.

Sources and references

The following is a list of some basic general sources by chapter, which will also serve as recommendations for further reading; together with precise citations for quotations. Numerical references are to page numbers.

Introduction

Earlier comparisons of British and American 'imperialisms' are Niall Ferguson's brilliant and provocative *Empire: How Britain Made the Modern World* (2003) and *Colossus: The Rise and Fall of the American Empire* (2004), taken both together; and Linda Colley's stimulating first thoughts on the subject, 'Some difficulties of Empire – past, present and future', *Common Knowledge*, vol. 11, no. 2 (2005), pp. 198–214.

Other references

1   Donald Rumsfeld: reported in *Guardian*, 2 March 2003.
4–5   Mark Steyn: 'Imperialism is the answer', comes from *Chicago Sun-Times*, 14 October 2001; Charles Krauthammer is quoted by Emily Eakin in '"It takes an empire," say several US thinkers', *New York Times*, 2 April 2002; David Frum is quoted in Jeet Heer, 'US takes on burden of empire', *National Post* (Canada), 29 March 2003; and the Max Boot quote comes from 'The case for American empire', *Weekly Standard*, 15 October 2001.
11   The 'conspiracy theory' linking modern American foreign policy with Cecil Rhodes was dreamt up by Carroll Quigley: *Tragedy and Hope: A History of the World in our Time* (1966) and *The Anglo-American Establishment* (1981).
13   The Kipling line comes from his poem 'The English flag' (1891).

Chapter 1   'Like a house of cards'

Much of this chapter summarises my own *The Lion's Share: A Short History of British Imperialism 1850–2004* (4th edn, 2004), where elaborations and explanations of most of the points made here, together with their sources, can be found. Other excellent general histories of modern British imperialism are Ronald Hyam, *Britain's Imperial Century* (2nd edn, 1993); Bill Nasson, *Britannia's Empire: Making a British World* (2004); and the new *Oxford History of the British Empire* (5 vols, 1998–9, plus supplements).

Other references

17 and passim   The evidence for British apathy towards empire among certain classes and at different times, mentioned at various points in this chapter, is presented in my *The Absent-minded Imperialists: Empire, Society and Culture in Britain* (2004).

24   Cobden: from speech in Manchester, 15 January 1846, in John Bright and Thorold Rogers (eds), *Speeches on Questions of Public Policy by Richard Cobden, MP* (1870), vol. 1, pp. 362–3.

26   Seeley: from *The Expansion of England* (1883), pp. 7–10.

27   The frightened 1909 imperialist is Walter Frewen Lord, 'The creed of imperialism', in *The Nineteenth Century*, vol. 66 (1909), p. 35.

27–8   The Belloc lines come from his poem 'The Modern Traveller' (1898).

29   The Emmanuel Todd reference is to his *After the Empire: The Breakdown of the American Order* (English translation, 2003).

31   The report referred to is *The Final Report of the Royal Commission on the Depression in Trade and Industry* (1886).

31   The Pfaff book was first published in 1989; this quote comes from the revised (2000) edn, p. 280.

33   Gladstone on German colonisation is quoted in W. L. Langer, *European Alliances and Alignments 1871–1890* (1931), p. 308.

37   The Chief of the General Staff worried about imperial vulnerability is Sir Henry Wilson, quoted in C. E. Callwell, *Field-Marshal Sir Henry Wilson* (1927), vol. 2, pp. 240–1.

37   For Hitler's hint of an offer to let Britain keep her empire (in 1935), see Ian Kershaw, *Hitler 1889–1936: Hubris* (1998), p. 556.

38   The Indian Brigadier-General on 'prestige' is one Surtees, quoted in Nigel Collett, *The Butcher of Amritsar: General Reginald Dyer* (2004), p. 384.

40   'Methods of barbarism': Sir Henry Campbell-Bannerman in House of Commons, 14 June 1901, quoted in J. A. Spender, *The Life of the Right Hon. Sir Henry Campbell-Bannerman* (n.d.), vol. 1, p. 336.

41 Balfour on the Middle East: quoted in A. P. Thornton, *The Imperial Idea and its Enemies* (1959), p. 168.

43 Churchill in 1942 ('King's First Minister') is quoted in Wm Roger Louis, *Imperialism at Bay* (1977), p. 200.

43 Enoch Powell offering to retake India is retailed (*via* R. A. Butler, an undependable source) by Patrick Cosgrave, *The Lives of Enoch Powell* (1989), p. 115.

46 Churchill on Natalians: see Ronald Hyam, *Elgin and Churchill at the Colonial Office, 1905–1908* (1965), p. 251.

47 On Hobson, see my *Critics of Empire* (1968), ch. 6.

51 On 'ornamentalism', see David Cannadine, *Ornamentalism: How the British Saw their Empire* (2001).

52 Wilberforce is quoted in Eric Stokes, *The English Utilitarians and India* (1959), p. 23; Macaulay in ibid., pp. 45–6.

53 The J. R. Green quote is from *A Short History of the English People* (1874), p. 818; Disraeli's wise words on the Indian Mutiny are in *Hansard's Parliamentary Debates*, 3rd series, vol. 147 (1867), cc. 440–80; and the Alfred Lyall quote is in Roger Owen, *Lord Cromer* (2004), p. 169.

53 Kipling's 'The White Man's Burden' was written in 1899.

58 Public schoolboys 'going bad' in the tropics: from the *Wellingtonian*, vol. 12, no. 1 (1898), p. 10.

59 'Mothball phase': H. Stephens, *The Political Development of Tanganyika* (1968), p. 30.

60 Furse on 'cleverness': see Anthony Kirk-Greene, *Britain's Colonial Administrators 1858–1966* (2000), p. 180.

Chapter 2   'Not colonies but outposts'

On American 'imperialism', as well as Niall Ferguson, *Colossus*, see Walter LaFeber, *The New Empire: An Interpretation of American Expansion 1860–1898* (1963); William Appleman Williams, *The Roots of Modern American Empire* (1969); V. G. Kiernan, *America: The New Imperialism* (1978); and Frank Ninkovich, *The United States and Imperialism* (2001).

Other references

62 Lawrence Summers on American non-imperialism: speech (as Deputy Secretary of US Treasury) to the 6th Annual Conference of the Americas, at the Waldorf-Astoria Hotel, New York, 9 October 1997.

64 The 'salt water fallacy': see Wm Roger Louis, *Imperialism at Bay* (1977), p. 570.

65   The Bostonian, Adams and Washington quotes are taken from Richard W. van Alstyne, *The American Empire: Its Historical Pattern and Evolution* (1960), pp. 9–10, 15.

67   William Appleman Williams, see *Roots of Modern American Empire.*

69   Frederick Jackson Turner's famous book was called *The Significance of the Frontier in American History* (1894).

69   The business journal was the *Banker's Magazine*, quoted in LaFeber, *The New Empire*, p. 20.

71   The Theodore Roosevelt quote about boa-constrictors and porcupines is taken from *The Theodore Roosevelt Web Book* (www.theodore roosevelt.org/TR%20Web%20Book), p. 550.

71   The first outing of Hobson's theory attributing imperialism to surplus capital was his 'Free trade and foreign policy', in *Contemporary Review*, August 1898; Conant's essay *advocating* imperialism on these grounds appeared in the *North American Review* in the following month.

73   Leopold Amery's statement on mandates can be found in *Hansard's Parliamentary Debates*, 5th series, vol. 118, col. 2175.

76   For Cordell Hull on British tariffs, see Allan M. Winkler, 'American opposition to imperialism during World War II', in Rhodri Jeffreys-Jones (ed.), *Eagle against Empire: American Opposition to European Imperialism, 1914–1982* (1983), p. 79.

78–82   These pages draw heavily on Wm Roger Louis, *Imperialism at Bay* (1977). The following quotes and references are taken from there: *Life* magazine October 1942: p. 198; FDR's dislike of British imperialism: p. 147; the 'mentality of 1776': p. 111; FDR's 1781 model for India, and Churchill's comment: pp. 149–50; the 'Sermon on the Mount' jibe (by Isaiah Bowman): p. 336; Hailey's point that Britain invented anti-imperialism: p. 206; Churchill's suggestion that the UN should inspect the American South: p. 357; Smuts's encomium to the Empire: p. 209; FDR on Gambia: p. 356; Churchill, 'Hands off the British Empire': p. 433; Stimson, not colonies but outposts: p. 484; the disagreement over the Atlantic Charter: pp. 123–9; and Churchill on not wanting to be put into the dock: p. 458.

82   The Colonial Secretary's (Oliver Stanley) pledge to the colonies was made on 13 July 1943; see *Hansard's Parliamentary Debates*, 5th series, vol. 391, col. 48.

84–5   The Dulles quote ('walking a tightrope') is taken from Wm Roger Louis and Ronald Robinson, 'The imperialism of decolonisation', *Journal of Imperial and Commonwealth History*, vol. 33, no. 3 (1994), p.480. The term 'imperial Anglo-Americanism' is also to be found there, on p. 470; and the point about the return to mid-Victorianism on p. 495.

88 The Emmanuel Todd book referred to here is *After the Empire*. Patrick O'Brien's argument is to be found in 'The governance of globalization: the political economy of Anglo-American hegemony, 1793–2003', CESIFO Working Paper no. 1023 (September 2003).

89 *The End of History and the Last Man* is the title of Francis Fukuyama's book (1992).

89 William E. Odom and Robert Dujarric, *America's Inadvertent Empire* (2004), p. 2 and endnote, refers to America's frequent support for terrorist movements (if they were anti-communist) in Afghanistan and elsewhere.

90 The figure of 702 US overseas bases comes from the Common Dreams News Center (www.commondreams.org), 26 June 2005, citing the US Defense Department's annual 'Base structure report' for the fiscal year 2003. Later estimates put it even higher.

90 The famous Eisenhower warning about the 'military-industrial complex' was given in his farewell broadcast address, 17 January 1961, printed in *Public Papers of the Presidents, Dwight D. Eisenhower* (1960), pp. 1035–1040.

Chapter 3   'We don't do empire'

The following is a very small selection of the many books devoted to the 'imperial' aspects of post-9/11 American foreign policy: Chalmers Johnson, *Blowback: The Costs and Consequences of American Empire* (2000); Andrew J. Bacevich, *American Empire: The Realities and Consequences of US Diplomacy* (2002); Robert Kagan, *Paradise and Power: America and Europe in the New World Order* (2003); and Clyde Prestowitz, *Rogue Nation: American Unilateralism and the Failure of Good Intentions* (2003).

Other references

93 The Cheney quote was reported in *New York Times*, 25 January 2004; the Bush one in the *Washington Post*, reprinted in *Guardian Weekly*, 29 January–4 February 2004; the Rice reference comes from Peter Beaumont, 'Now for the Bush Doctrine', *Observer*, 22 September 2003.

94 Dinesh d'Souza's article was in *Christian Science Monitor*, 26 April 2002.

96 Condoleezza Rice's early statement of her foreign policy objectives appeared as an article entitled 'Promoting the national interest', in *Foreign Affairs*, January/February 2000.

96   The Project for the New American Century's website is www.newamericancentury.org. The phrase 'full spectrum dominance' was coined in a US Department of Defense paper, *Joint Vision 2020*, in 2000.

99   Chalmers Johnson: see his *Blowback* (new edn, 2002).

99   On the *London Review of Books* row, see the issues of 4 October (Mary Beard), and 18 October (letters page), 2001.

102   The Winthrop sermon, entitled 'A modell of Christian charity', is taken from the Hanover Historical Texts Project, to be found at http://history.hanover.edu/texts/winthmod. html.

102   I got the Jefferson quote from Michael Ignatieff, 'Who are the Americans to think that freedom is theirs to spread?', *New York Times*, 26 June 2005; the Franklin quote from Robert Kagan, *Paradise and Power: America and Europe in the New World Order*, p. 88; and the Wilson quote from Andrew Bacevich, *American Empire*, p. 425; but these are oft-quoted.

103   Reagan's 'last best hope' comes from his Second Inaugural Address, 21 January 1985 (though he took it from Abraham Lincoln, referring in his case to 'liberty'); the Madeleine Albright statement was made on NBC's *Today* show, 19 February 1998; Condoleezza Rice's *dicta* are taken from the *Foreign Affairs* article cited already; for Clinton on 'history', see Bacevich, *American Empire*, p. 34; Bush's claim about God and history was made in a speech to B'nai Brith International (a Jewish human rights organisation) on 28 August 2000.

106–7 The Bacevich quote is in his *American Empire*, p. 218; the 'soft power' term is Joseph Nye's: see his *Soft Power: The Means to Success in World Politics* (2004), and earlier works.

108   President Bush's second inaugural address was delivered on 20 January 2005.

108–9 The McKinley (1900) and Woodrow Wilson quotes here both come from John B. Judis, *The Folly of Empire* (2004), p. 4; the Beveridge quote (1898) is taken from James Andrew and David Zarefsky, *American Voices: Significant Speeches in American History, 1640–1945* (1989), pp. 374–8.

109   'Democracies never go to war': see Spencer R. Weart, *Never at War: Why Democracies will not Fight One Another* (1997); on Leo Strauss, see Anne Norton, *Leo Strauss and the Politics of American Empire* (2004).

109   The definition of 'fascism' appears – further elaborated – in Robert Paxton, *The Anatomy of Fascism* (2004), p. 218.

110   Michael Northcott's book is *An Angel Directs the Storm: Apocalyptic Religion and American Empire* (2004). The direct quote is on p. 6.

112 On 'madness' in American politics, see Richard Hofstadter, *The Paranoid Style in American Politics* (1965).

113 Anatol Lieven's book is *America Right or Wrong: An Anatomy of American Nationalism* (2004).

114 I have not been able to find a direct source for the 'Ambrose Bierce' witticism; only attributions to him.

116 On the oil 'conspiracy', see 'Retort', 'Blood for oil?', *London Review of Books*, 21 April 2005, p. 12.

117 The Jay Garner interview was on BBC News (world edn), 15 April 2003; the Cheney interview ('we will be greeted as liberators') on NBC's *Meet the Press*, 16 March 2003.

119 America's 'colonial problem': see Andrew Bacevich, *American Empire*, p. 243.

120 On the place of war in American history, see Fred Anderson and Andrew Cayton, *The Dominion of War: Empire and Conflict in North America 1500–2000* (2005).

120 David Rieff is quoted in Tony Judt, 'The New World Order', in *New York Review of Books*, 14 July 2005 (from Rieff's *At the Point of a Gun: Democratic Dreams and Armed Intervention*, 2005).

121 Graham Greene, *The Quiet American* (1955); the quotes are taken from the Vintage edn (2002), pp. 20, 96.

121 Rumsfeld's 'old Europe' remarks were reported on CNN World News, 23 January 2003.

123 The Ignatieff quote is from 'Who are Americans to think that freedom is theirs to spread?', cited already.

124 Bush on 'respect for women' comes in his State of the Union Address, 29 January 2002.

128 Joseph Nye on 'rotting from within', in *The Paradox of American Power* (2002), p. 111.

129 Paul Kennedy's 'overstretch' idea is elaborated in his *The Rise and Fall of the Great Powers* (1987). One of a number of criticisms of it after the fall of the Soviet Union was Henry R. Nau, 'Why "The Rise and Fall of the Great Powers" was wrong', *Review of International Studies*, vol. 27 (2001).

Chapter 4   'Still a global player'

On Tony Blair's foreign policy, see John Kampfner, *Blair's Wars* (2003); Anthony Seldon, *Blair* (2004); James Naughtie, *The Accidental American: Tony Blair and the Presidency* (2004); and Philip Stephens, *Tony Blair: The Price of Leadership* (2004).

Other references

135   The Martin Jacques article, 'The age of selfishness', appeared in the *Guardian*, 5 October 2002.

135   Dean Acheson was speaking at the West Point Military Academy, 5 December 1962.

135   Prince Harry's 'Colonials and Natives' party was held at Olympic show jumper Richard Meade's country estate in Wiltshire on 8 January 2005; the pictures were published in the *Sun* newspaper on 13 January.

136   The 1948 survey is entitled *Public Opinion on Colonial Affairs*, and was compiled by G. K. Evens for the Colonial Office.

138   Empire 'rehabilitations': see for example Robert Rhodes James, 'Now that the sun has gone down', *The Times*, 3 November 1995.

140   The Hailey quote comes from Wm Roger Louis, *Imperialism at Bay*, p. 51.

142   The Salisbury quote (1887) can be found in Lady Gwendolen Cecil, *Life of Robert, Marquis of Salisbury*, vol. 4, *1887–1892* (1932), p. 65.

143   'The last country on the planet' is from Seamus Milne, 'Throwing our weight about', in *Guardian*, 11 September 2000.

143–4   Jack Straw's criticisms of the British Empire appear in the *New Statesman*, 18 November 2002 (flagged on BBC Radio, 15 November). The 'old fogey' response is in the letters columns of the *Daily Telegraph*, 16 November. Blair's intention to mention the Empire in his 1997 Manchester speech is mentioned in Kampfner, *Blair's Wars*, p. 4. Brown's 2005 remarks were reported in the *Daily Mail*, 15 January 2005.

144–5   The Home Office booklet was entitled *Life in the United Kingdom: A Journey to Citizenship*.

146   Foreign aid figures are published in the UK government's annual *Statistics on International Development*.

146   'Britain's colonial burden returning': Kampfner, *Blair's Wars*, p. 71.

146–7   The Blair speeches quoted here were delivered to the Lord Mayor's banquet, 11 November 1997, quoted in Kampfner, *Blair's Wars*, p. 17; and at the Partnership Summit in Bangalore, 5 January 2002, formerly reproduced on the internet at www.meadev.nic.in/speeches/ps-tony-5jan.htm.

148   The 'cynics' quote (February 2002) comes from Kampfner, *Blair's Wars*, p. 77; the 'good/bad' one (1993) from Paul Richards (ed.), *Tony Blair in his Own Words* (2004), p. 73.

149–50   The pivotal Chicago speech (22 April 1999) can be found on the internet at www.pbs.org/newshour/bb/international/ jan-june99/blair_doctrine4–23.html.

150–1 For Cabinet and Foreign Office doubts about the Iraq War, see 'From memos, insights into ally's doubts on Iraq War', *Washington Post*, 28 June 2005.

153 The 'fucking crazies' expression is reported in the *Guardian*, 12 September 2004; Blair on the fuss about the Neocons in James Naughtie, *The Accidental American*, p. 71.

155 Bolton's 'no such thing as the UN' is quoted widely, from a speech at a Federalist Forum, 1994.

157 'Africa doesn't pay': Bacevich, *American Empire*, p. 111.

158 For Rumsfeld's 'thirty days', see Niall Ferguson, 'Cowboys and Indians', *New York Times*, 24 May 2005.

158 Blair couldn't get Bush to 'focus' on Iraqi reconstruction: Kampfner, *Blair's Wars*, p. 316. 'The morning after' is David Manning (Foreign Office), from documents reproduced in the *Washington Post*, 28 June 2005.

158–9 Martin Wolf's article is in the *Financial Times*, 10 December 2001; Max Boot's is in *Weekly Standard*, 15 October 2001; the Ferguson 'timetable' quote is from 'Cowboys and Indians', cited above.

Conclusion

References

167 For Samuel Huntington, see his *The Clash of Civilizations and the Remaking of World Order* (1996).

167 For predictions of British imperial decline, see my 'The Edwardians and their empire', in Donald Read (ed.), *Edwardian England* (1982).

169 The Sri Lankan commentary was an article entitled 'The bare doctrine of Blair the bear', *Kalaya*, 28 April 1999.

170 Ferguson's 'seventy years' prognosis is in 'Cowboys and Indians', cited above.

172 Imperialism by invitation: see Geir Lundestad, 'Empire by invitation? The United States and Western Europe, 1945–1952', *Journal of Peace Research*, 23 (September 1986).

174 Blaming the British Empire for Jamaican homophobia: see Jeremy Seabrook, 'It's not natural', *Guardian*, 3 July 2004.

174–5 The India–Vietnam comparison appears in a 'blog' called 'Chapati mystery' (www. chapatimystery.com), posted by 'Vagabond' on 9 June 2005.

176 The V. I. Lenin work referred to is *Imperialism, the Highest Stage of Capitalism* (English translation, 1922).

178–80 MacDonald's colonial philosophy is elaborated in my *Critics of Empire: British Radical Attitudes to Colonialism in Africa*

1895–1914 (1968), pp. 185–9, where the original sources for these quotations can be found.

182   Rosebery's 'fly-blown phylactery' is also in my *Critics of Empire*, p. 79.

183   Sumner Welles is quoted in Wm Roger Louis, *Imperialism at Bay*, pp. 154–5.

Index